D1227244

A CHILD
GROWING UP

To Chad,

On page 40 there's a
story written by Stuart aged 12.
Why not send me one of yours

David Kerry

A CHILD GROWING UP

A Journey Through the Bittersweet Joys of Childhood Experience

Collection by David Kemp
Illustrations by Klaas van Weringh

 Simon & Pierre
Toronto, Ontario, Canada

We would like to express our gratitude to The Canada Council and the Ontario Arts Council for their support.

Marian M. Wilson, Publisher

© 1979 by David Kemp
All rights reserved

No portion of this book may be reproduced or transmitted in any form or by any means, including photocopying except for brief passages in the context of a review, without the written permission of the publisher.

The Acknowledgments are a continuation of the copyright page.

54321 • 32109

Canadian Cataloguing in Publication Data
Main entry under title:
A Child Growing Up
ISBN 0-88924-103-1 pa.
1. Children — Literary collections. I . Kemp, David, 1936 —
PN6071.C5C48   808.8'0352   C79-094643-2
PZ5.C485

Editor: Marian M. Wilson

Typesetting: Type Master
Printer: Johanns Graphics Ltd.
Cover Drawing: Klaas van Weringh

Simon & Pierre Publishing Company Limited
Order Department: P.O. Box 280, Adelaide Street Postal Station
Toronto, Ontario, Canada M5C 2J4

Printed and bound in Canada.

*This anthology is dedicated
to Lisa*

My thanks to
Marian Wilson — for faith
Margaret Koen — for typing
My Parents — for their help and encouragement
and to
the Permissions Editors, authors and
translators — for their understanding

Introduction

Apart from birth, which few of us remember, and death, which we try not to think about, the most universally shared human experience is, in all probability, that of childhood.

Most of us recall our childhood with nostalgia, delight and sentimentality. I sometimes suspect that our recollections are almost exclusively concerned with pleasure while managing to block those painful memories which we all have stored away. Whatever the mix of pleasure and sorrow we give to our active memories, it is certain that the experiences behind them are of inestimable importance. The shape of our childhood is the most crucial factor in determining the shape of our adulthood.

Childhood is really the miracle of growing up. We feel this miracle most poignantly in the form of a lament, for as we approach maturity, a sense of regret and sadness accompanies us on our journey. It is a sadness brought about by the realisation that "nothing ever stands still and that things are changing all the time."

A Child Growing Up is a journey through the bittersweet world of childhood memory. In it, we recall the key of the kingdom of the imagination in which Matilda shouts "Fire!" once too often and in which Oliver Twist timidly asks for more. There are recollections too of the first day at school, a poverty stricken Christmas and the death of a son. The final image, the holiness of childhood, is a quietly persuasive comment on the feelings of loss that come with adulthood.

In *A Child Growing Up,* as in childhood itself, the mood is at times gay and carefree, at times darkened by cynicism and gloom. There is comedy, anger, joy, puzzlement, and pathos. Above all, I hope that there is honesty and authenticity, for it is on this base that each reader will be able to understand his own indentification, indeed his own journey, into the valued moments of a time that will never truly be recaptured. While we, unlike Peter Pan, must each of us face the day when the miracle of growing up is but a memory, much is lost to us even in adulthood if we fail to treasure at least some of the qualities of childhood.

This book is meant to be enjoyed. My personal wish is that it will also be cherished for what it can tell us about ourselves.

David Kemp

7 **Introduction** by David Kemp

Prologue
    11 **Prayer Before Birth** by Louis MacNeice

Childhood Innocence
    14 **When I Was Young,** translated from the Eskimo by
            Knud Rasmussen
       Cradle Song, by Walter Scott
    15 **Lullabye of the Iroquois,** translated from the Iroquois
            by E. Pauline Johnson (Tekahionwake)
    16 **High Heels** by Raymond Souster
    17 **Innocence** by Irving Layton
    18 **The Key of the Kingdom** by Ed Reed

Children and Parents
    22 **Father** by Dale Zieroth
    23 **Song to be Sung by the Father of Infant Female Children**
            by Ogden Nash
    25 **My Son! And What's a Son?,** attributed to Ben Jonson from
            The Spanish Tragedy by Thomas Kyd
    26 **Do You Laugh or Cry?** excerpt from *Ten Lost Years* by
            Barry Broadfoot
    27 **Keine Lazarovitch 1870 - 1959** by Irving Layton
    28 **Before Two Portraits of My Mother** by Emile Nelligan,
            translated from the French by George Johnston
    29 **Model Parents** by Eloi de Grandmont, translated from the
            French by John Glassco

Child Death
    32 **Concerning This Child** by Hector St.-Denys Garneau,
            translated from the French by Jean Beaupré and Gael
            Turnbull
    33 **Death of a Young Son by Drowning** by Margaret Atwood
    34 **Death of a Son (who died in a mental hospital, aged one)** by
            Jon Silkin
    35 **Brian on the Hillside,** excerpt from *Ten Lost Years*
            by Barry Broadfoot

Children At Play
    38 **Boy Playing with Mud** by Raymond Souster
       I Was Around Six by George Jonas
    39 **The Children Are Laughing** by Gwendolyn MacEwen
    40 **The Dog With a Million Fleas** by Stuart Widdows (aged 12)

Children And School
    44 **First Day,** excerpt from *Clearing in the West* by Nellie McClung
    45 **Village School,** excerpt from *Cider With Rosie* by Laurie Lee
    46 **Timothy Winters** by Charles Causley
    47 **Exercise Book** by Jacques Prévert, translated from the French
            by Paul Dehn
    48 **Excerpt from** *Oliver Twist* by Charles Dickens

50 **A Boy's Head** by Miroslav Holub, translated from the Czech
    by Ian Milner
51 **About School,** Anonymous
52 **The School Globe** by James Reaney

Children And Make Believe

56 **Legend** by Judith Wright
57 **maggie and milly and molly and may** by e.e. cummings
58 **Excerpt from** *Portrait of the Artist As A Young Dog* by
    Dylan Thomas
59 **I, Icarus** by Alden Nowlan
    And What If by Gael Turnbull
60 **A Backwards Journey** by P.K. Page
61 **The Unicorn** by Mary Oliver

Children and Relatives

64 **Roots** by Alden Nowlan
66 **The Night Grandma Died** by Elizabeth Brewster
67 **The Bratty Brother (Sister)** by Dennis Lee
    A Grandfather by Florence McNeil
69 **Grandfather** by George Bowering

Children At Christmas

72 **Excerpt from** *Cameos of Pioneer Life in Western Canada*
        by Kate Johnson
73 **Parade of the Toys** by Raymond Souster
74 **Excerpt from** A Child's Christmas in Wales by Dylan Thomas
76 **Excerpt from** *Act One* by Moss Hart
78 **Excerpt from** *Who Has Seen The Wind* by W.O. Mitchell

Advice To Children

84 **Enfant** by Jacques Godbout, translated from the French by
        John Robert Colombo
    Report, Anonymous
87 **First Lesson** by Phyllis McGinley
    Matilda by Hilaire Belloc
89 **Advice to the Young** by Miriam Waddington

Child Love

92 **An Ounce of Cure** by Alice Munro
101 **First Bite at the Apple,** excerpt from *Cider With Rosie*
        by Laurie Lee

The Holy Child

104 **The Selfish Giant** by Oscar Wilde

109 **Author Biographies**

125 **Acknowledgments**

Prayer Before Birth

I am not yet born; O hear me.
Let not the bloodsucking bat or the rat or the stoat of the
    clubfooted ghoul come near me.

I am not yet born; console me.
I fear that the human race may with tall walls wall me,
    with strong drugs dope me, with wise lies lure me,
        on black racks rack me, in blood-baths roll me.

I am not yet born; provide me
With water to dandle me, grass to grow from me, trees to talk
    to me, sky to sing to me, birds and a white light
        In the back of my mind to guide me.

I am not yet born; forgive me.
For the sins that in me the world shall commit, my words
    when they speak me, my thoughts when they think me,
        my treason engendered by traitors beyond me,
            my life when they murder by means of my
                hands, my death when they live me.

I am not yet born; release me
In the parts I must play and the cues I must take when
    old men lecture me, bureaucrats hector me, mountains
        frown at me, lovers laugh at me, the white
            waves call me to folly and the desert calls
                me to doom and the beggar refuses
                    my gift and my children curse me.

I am not yet born; O hear me,
Let not the man who is beast or who thinks he is God come
    near me.

I am not yet born; O fill me
With strength against those who would freeze my
    humanity, would dragoon me into a lethal automaton,
        would make me a cog in a machine, a thing with
            one face, a thing, and against all those
                who would dissipate my entirety, would
                    blow me like thistledown hither and
                        thither or hither and thither
                            like water held in the
                                hands would spill me.
Let them not make me a stone and let them not spill me.
Otherwise kill me.

Louis MacNeice

Childhood Innocence

The Key of the Kingdom

When I was Young

When I was young,
every day was a beginning
of some new thing,
and every evening ended
with a glow of the next day's dawn.

Translated from the Eskimo by **Knud Rasmussen**

Cradle Song

O hush thee, my baby, thy sire was a knight,
Thy mother a lady, both lovely and bright;
The woods and the glens, from the towers which we see,
They all are belonging, dear baby, to thee.

O fear not the bugle, though loudly it blows,
It calls but the warders that guard thy repose;
Their bows would be bended, their blades would be red,
Ere the step of a foeman draws near to thy bed.

O hush thee, my baby, the time will soon come,
When thy sleep shall be broken by trumpet and drum;
Then hush thee, my darling, take rest while you may,
For strife comes with manhood, and waking with day.

Walter Scott

Lullaby of the Iroquois

Little brown baby-bird, lapped in your nest,
    Wrapped in your nest,
    Strapped in your nest,
Your straight little cradle-board rocks you to rest,
    Its hands are your nest,
    Its bands are your nest.
It swings from the down-bending branch of the oak,
You watch the camp flame, and the curling gray smoke,
But, oh, for your pretty black eyes sleep is best,
Little brown baby of mine, go to rest.

Little brown baby-bird swinging to sleep,
    Winging to sleep,
    Singing to sleep,
Your wonder-black eyes that so wide open keep,
    Shielding their sleep,
    Unyielding to sleep.
The heron is homing, the plover is still,
The night owl calls from his haunt on the hill,
Afar the fox barks, afar the stars peep,
Little brown baby of mine, go to sleep.

Translated from the Iroquois by **E. Pauline Johnson (Tekahionwake)**

High Heels

Little girl from next door
in your mother's high heels
oceans too big for you,
yet managing somehow
to edge down the sidewalk.

Too soon you'll have
a pair all your own
to show off those legs,
leaving childhood behind
with the kindling shape of them.

Right now I want
those small running feet
with the silk hair above,
the face full of wonder.

You'll be old soon enough,
your beauty a trouble
to all those who see you,
your manner self-conscious,
so terribly proud,

little girl going by
with the click-clack-clatter
of your mother's heels
walking hard on my heart.

Raymond Souster

Innocence

how does one tell
one's fourteen-year-old daughter
that the beautiful
are the most vulnerable
and that a rage
tears at the souls
of humans
to corrupt innocence
and to smash butterflies
to see their wings
flutter in the sun
pulling weeds and flowers
from the soil:
and that all, all
go under the earth
to make room for more
weeds and flowers
— some more beautiful than others?

Irving Layton

The Key of the Kingdom

When we were children
We possessed the key to a kingdom
Such as this world has yet to see.
Wherever we went,
By lakes,
Pools
And streams,
In woods,
Meadows
And fields,
There was a world beyond belief
In which anything could be something else.
A world
Whose every corner
Would yield some new adventure or surprise.
A world
In which we ruled
And was ours alone,

Only we children had the key,
The key of the kingdom.

A world inhabited by goblins, ghosts and ghouls,
Dragons, trolls, witches, sorcerers,
Knights, fair damsels, wicked kings
And green-skinned, three-eyed floops.
A world of enchanted geography —
Magic forests,
Glass mountains
And fountains of youth.

In this world
We held our castles
Made of T.V. boxes
Against marauding bands of Vikings
Armed with swords made of lattice
And shields taken from the tops of garbage cans.
We sailed with Columbus
Across the unchartered waters of a lily pond.
We descended
With Captain Nemo
To 20,000 leagues beneath the bathwater.
We went west with the pioneers
By coaster wagon,
And to the East with Marco Polo
By tricycle.

We defied savage Indians
From the next block
And returned alive
In time for an afternoon nap.
We hunted fierce man-eating squirrels.
We dared damnation
By taking the trainer wheels
Off our first bicycle.
We did a zillion billion other brave
Courageous
Bold
Fun things.

Now that we are older
Wiser
And more mature
This kingdom no longer has our allegiance.
We have lost the key
And it has perished with the rust of misuse
And neglect.

Age is the graveyard
Of all our youthful hopes
Dreams
And experiences.

Ed Reed

Children and Parents

Ten Lost Years

Father

Twice he took me in his hands and shook
me like a sheaf of wheat, the way a dog shakes
a snake, as if he meant to knock out my tongue
and grind it under his heel right there
on the kitchen floor. I never remembered
what he said or the warnings he gave; she
always told me afterwards, when he
had left and I had stopped my crying. I
was eleven that year and for seven more years
I watched his friends laughing and him
with his great hands rising and falling
with every laugh, smashing down on his knees
and making the noise of a tree when it cracks
in winter. Together they drank chokecherry
wine and talked of dead friends and the
old times when they were young and because
I never thought of getting old, their
youth was the first I knew of dying.

Sunday before church he would trim
his fingernails with the hunting knife
his East German cousins had sent, the same
knife he used for castrating pigs and
skinning deer: things that had nothing
to do with Sunday. Communion once
a month, a shave every third day, a
good chew of snuff, these were the things
that helped a man to stand in the sun for
eight hours a day, to sweat through each
cold hailstorm without a word, to freeze
fingers and feet to cut wood in winter, to do
the work that bent his back a little more
each day down toward the ground.

Last Christmas, for the first time, he
gave presents, unwrapped and bought
with pension money. He drinks mostly coffee
now, sleeping late and shaving everyday.
Even the hands have changed: white, soft,
unused hands. Still he seems content
to be this old, to be sleeping in the middle
of the afternoon with his mouth open as if there
is no further need for secrets, as if he is
no longer afraid to call his children fools
for finding different answers, different lives.

Dale Zieroth

Song to be Sung by the Father of Infant Female Children

My heart leaps up when I behold
A rainbow in the sky;
Contrariwise, my blood runs cold
When little boys go by.
For little boys as little boys,
No special hate I carry,
But now and then they grow to men,
And when they do, they marry.
No matter how they tarry,
Eventually they marry.
And, swine among the pearls,
They marry little girls.

Oh, somewhere, somewhere, an infant plays,
With parents who feed and clothe him.
Their lips are sticky with pride and praise,
But I have begun to loathe him.
Yes, I loathe with a loathing shameless
This child who to me is nameless.
This bachelor child in his carriage
Gives never a thought to marriage,
But a person can hardly say knife
Before he will hunt him a wife.

I never see an infant (male),
A-sleeping in the sun,
Without I turn a trifle pale
And think is *he* the one?
Oh, first he'll want to crop his curls,
And then he'll want a pony,
And then he'll think of pretty girls
And holy matrimony.
He'll put away his pony,
And sigh for matrimony.
A cat without a mouse
Is he without a spouse.

Oh, somewhere he bubbles bubbles of milk,
And quietly sucks his thumbs;
His cheeks are roses painted on silk,
And his teeth are tucked in his gums.
But alas, the teeth will begin to grow,
And the bubbles will cease to bubble;
Given a score of years or so,
The roses will turn to stubble.
He'll send a bond, or he'll write a book,

And his eyes will get that acquisitive look,
And raging and ravenous for the kill,
He'll boldly ask for the hand of Jill.
This infant whose middle
Is diapered still
Will want to marry
My daughter Jill.

Oh sweet be his slumber and moist his middle!
My dreams, I fear, are infanticiddle.
A fig for embryo Lohengrins!
I'll open all of his safety pins,
I'll pepper his powder and salt his bottle,
And give him readings from Aristotle,
Sand for his spinach I'll gladly bring,
And an elegant, elegant alligator
To play with in his perambulator.
Then perhaps he'll struggle through fire and water
To marry somebody else's daughter!

Ogden Nash

My Son! And What's A Son?

My son! and what's a son? A thing begot
Within a pair of minutes — thereabout;
A lump bred up in darkness, and doth serve
To ballast these light creatures we call women;
And, at nine months' end, creeps forth to light.
What is there yet in a son,
To make a father dote, rave, or run mad?
Being born, it pouts, cries, and breeds teeth.
What is there yet in a son? He must be fed,
Be taught to go, and speak. Ay, or yet
Why might not a man love a calf as well?
Or melt in passion o'er a frisking kid,
As for a son? Methinks, a young bacon,
Or a fine little smooth horse colt,
Should move a man as much as doth a son;
For one to these, in very little time,
Will grow to some good use; whereas a son,
The more he grows in stature, and in years,
The more unsquar'd, unbevell'd, he appears,
Reckons his parents among the rank of fools,
Strikes care upon their heads with his mad riots;
Makes them look old, before they meet with age.
This is a son! — And what a loss were this,
Consider'd truly? — O, but my Horatio
Grew out of reach of these insatiate humours:
He lov'd his loving parents;
He was my comfort, and his mother's joy,
The very arm that did hold up our house;
Our hopes were stored up in him,
None but a damned murderer could hate him ...
Well, heaven is heaven still!
And there is Nemesis, and Furies,
And things call'd whips,
And they sometimes do meet with murderers:
They do not always 'scape, that is some comfort.
Ay, ay, ay; and then time steals on,
And steals, and steals, till violence leaps forth
Like thunder wrapped in a ball of fire,
And so doth bring confusion to them all.

Attributed to **Ben Jonson** from
The Spanish Tragedy by **Thomas Kyd**

Do You Laugh Or Cry?

"We lived on Lind Street in Toronto and I think everybody but my Dad was out of work on our block. In the summer they'd just sit on their porches, arms folded, and wait for something to happen but nothing ever did.

There was the little man living a few doors down the street from us. Yes you'd have to say he was a nothing, the type that never said anything much. You know. It was six miles downtown to where the unemployment offices were and you had to get there about six in the morning to have any chance of a job, so this guy would get up about 4:30, winter or summer, and down he'd trudge, day after day, but it seemed he never could get a job. Then he'd walk home.

One day he came home about 7:30 at night, walking as usual, but somehow he'd got a job. He'd made five dollars that day and he let everybody know it. I guess you could say he was the proudest man in Toronto that day, and he sent his girl, about ten or so, down to the nearest store to buy two quarts of ice cream and some other small stuff. There was going to be a celebration.

But somehow, on the way back between the store and the house she lost the change. Don't ask me how it could happen. She just lost the change. You could see it in pantomine, her father gesturing on the front walk and the girl going through the little pocket of her dress and looking into the bag, but the money was gone.

Now here's a man who apparently never got mad, but he lost his cool. He started to thrash that kid right on the front yard. Hit her, push her, hit her again, screaming all the time, and the girl just stood there and took it.

Oh sure, all the men in the neighbourhood saw this, but they could figure out what had happened. Usually if they saw a man beating a child, two or three of them would go over and plough him. Not this time. They just sat there.

Finally the guy threw himself full length on the steps and started to cry. Sobbing. Hard. The first time he'd made any money by his own labor in maybe three or four years and it was gone. He cried, big sobs. And you know who went to comfort him? The little girl. She went over and sat beside him and spoke to him and put her hand on his shoulder.

Christ, you don't know whether to laugh or cry."

Excerpt from *Ten Lost Years* by **Barry Broadfoot**

Keine Lazarovitch
1870 — 1959

When I saw my mother's head on the cold pillow,
Her white waterfalling hair in the cheek's hollows,
I thought, quietly circling my grief, of how
She had loved God but cursed extravagantly his creatures.

For her final mouth was not water but a curse,
A small black hole, a black rent in the universe,
Which damned the green earth, stars and trees in its stillness
And the inescapable lousiness of growing old.

And I record she was comfortless, vituperative,
Ignorant, glad, and much else besides; I believe
She endlessly praised her black eyebrows, their thick weave,
Till plagiarizing Death leaned down and took them for his mould.

And spoiled a dignity I shall not again find,
And the fury of her stubborn limited mind;
Now none will shake her amber beads and call God blind,
Or wear them upon a breast so radiantly.

O fierce she was, mean and unaccommodating;
But I think now of the toss of her gold earrings,
Their proud carnal assertion, and her youngest sings
While all the rivers of her red veins move into the sea.

Irving Layton

Before Two Portraits of my Mother

I love the beautiful young girl of this
portrait, my mother, painted years ago
when her forehead was white, and there was no
shadow in the dazzling Venetian glass

of her gaze. But this other likeness shows
the deep trenches across her forehead's white
marble. The rose poem of her youth that
her marriage sang is far behind. Here is

my sadness: I compare these portraits, one
of a joy-radiant brow, the other care-
heavy: sunrise — and the thick coming on

of night. And yet how strange my ways seem,
for when I look at these faded lips my heart
smiles, but at the smiling girl my tears start.

Emile Nelligan
Translated from the French by *George Johnston*

Model Parents

There are parents who punish their children.
Others who scold them
Bother them
Badger them
Lecture them
Sicken them
Break them in
Cut them off
Keep them under and
Pull their ears.

Others who reason with them
Jaw them
Worry them
Confine them, bore
Them to death, chide

Them, chivy
Them, crush
Them, curse
Them and disinherit them.

There are also parents who chastise them.
Parents who pinch them
Strike them
Slap them
Spank them
Torment them
Knock them around
Smash them to bits
Hand them over to the Social Welfare and then
Go to bed and make others.

Then there are the ones who
Take away their dessert, keep them
From sleeping, forbid
Them to go out, cut off
Their pocket money, tell them to
Shut up.

Finally, there are those who give them
A good swift kick in the pants and a
Father's blessing on New Year's Day.

Eloi de Grandmont
Translated from the French by *John Glassco*

Child Death

Ten Lost Years

Concerning This Child

Concerning this child who didn't want to die
And of whom we have cherished at least the likeness like a portrait in a
    picture-frame in a living-room.
It's possible that we could be tremendously mistaken on his account.
He was perhaps not made for the high priesthood as we believed
He was perhaps only a child like others
And high only for our lowliness
And luminous only for our great shadow without anything at all
(Let's bury him, with the picture-frame and all).

He has brought us here like a squirrel which loses us behind him in the
    forest
And our care and our cunning were completely wasted seeking obstinately
    in the underbrush.
Our eyes were completely unnerved seeking his leap in the underbrush.

Our whole soul was lost lying in ambush for his passing which has lost us
We thought to discover the new world in the light of his eyes
We believed that he was going to return us to the lost paradise.

But now let's bury him, at least the picture-frame with the likeness
And all the tentative paths we have beaten down in his pursuit
And all the inviting traps we have set to catch him.

Hector Saint - Denys Garneau
Translated from The French by *Jean Beaupré* and *Gael Turnbull*

Death of a Young Son by Drowning

He, who navigated with success
the dangerous river of his own birth
once more set forth

on a voyage of discovery
into the land I floated on
but could not touch to claim.

His feet slid on the bank,
the currents took him:
he swirled with ice and trees in the swollen water

and plunged into distant regions,
his head a bathysphere;
through his eyes' thin glass bubbles

he looked out, reckless adventurer
on a landscape stranger than Uranus
we have all been to and some remember.

There was an accident; the air locked,
he was hung in the river like a heart.
They retrieved the swamped body,

cairn of my plans and future charts,
with poles and hooks
from among the nudging logs.

It was spring, the sun kept shining, the new grass
lept to solidity;
my hands glistened with details.

After the long trip I was tired of waves.
My foot hit rock. The dreamed sails
collapsed, ragged.

> I planted him in this country
> like a flag.

Margaret Atwood

Death of a Son
(who died in a mental hospital, aged one)

Something has ceased to come along with me.
Something like a person: something very like one.
   And there was no nobility in it
      Or anything like that.

Something was there like a one-year-
Old house, dumb as stone. While the near buildings
   Sang like birds and laughed
      Understanding the pact

They were to have with silence. But he
Neither sang nor laughed. He did not bless silence
   Like bread, with words.
      He did not forsake silence.

But rather, like a house in mourning
Kept the eye turned in to watch the silence while
   The other houses like birds
      Sang around him.

And the breathing silence neither
Moved nor was still.

I have seen stones: I have seen brick
But this house was made up of neither bricks nor stone
   But a house of flesh and blood
      With flesh of stone

And bricks for blood. A house
Of stones and blood in breathing silence with the other
   Birds singing crazy on its chimneys.
      But this was silence,

This was something else, this was
Hearing and speaking though he was a house drawn
   Into silence, this was
      Something religious in his silence,

Something shining in his quiet,
This was different this was altogether something else:
   Though he never spoke, this
      Was something to do with death.

And then slowly the eye stopped looking
Inward. The silence rose and became still.

The look turned to the outer place and stopped,
   With the birds still shrilling around him.
      And as if he could speak

He turned over on his side with this one year
Red as a wound
He turned over as if he could be sorry for this
And out of his eyes two great tears rolled, like stones, and he
        died.

Jon Silkin

Brian On The Hillside

"Our first baby died, little Brian, and we never did know from what. We'd gone north of Prince George to homestead and we hardly had a bean and the baby died within three days. Just turned blue and stayed that way until he died. I couldn't get out to a doctor because the wife was sick, too, so I tried the doctoring myself.

I made a little coffin and we put little Brian in it and as there were no cemeteries around anywhere, my wife and I decided to walk to a bluff looking out over the river where you could see a long way and it was peaceful. I carried the coffin on my shoulder and my wife carried the shovel and when we got there I dug the little grave and pounded in, no, I planted four small saplings, at each corner, and then we both said the Lord's Prayer, and I guess you could say that was that.

In a few days the road dried up enough you could get over it and as the wife seemed to be worsening I hitched up the team and drove her into town. The doctor was a decent sort and he gave her some medicine, didn't charge us for a big bottle. Just before we left he asked where the baby was and I said he had died and we'd buried him. The doctor said that was too bad, how sorry he was, and we went back home.

About a week later a policeman came to the shack and this man was a son of a bitch. He was all set to throw me in jail, not reporting a death, unlawfully disposing of a dead body, a lot of nonsense. I said to him that little Brian was peaceful out on that hillside, and my wife was crying by this time, and I said that if he didn't get off my property there was going to be one less policeman in this country. He left. In fact, he got out real quick and I expected to hear something more about that, threatening a policeman or something, but I never did. Not a word.

Those saplings must be real tall trees now. That was a long time ago."

Excerpt from *Ten Lost Years* by **Barry Broadfoot**

Children at Play

I Was Around Six

Boy Playing With Mud

No baker ever kneaded more lovingly
bread-roll or loaf than this boy
in the early sun mixing his mud ball
back and forth, one hand to the other,
not worrying what he can make of it,
the feeling of roundness, of wetness,
of sand in his palms and on his fingers
enough for him and his child's mood,
and me, and this whole
lazy summer morning.

Raymond Souster

I Was Around Six

                         I was around six
When another little boy
Punched me in the nose without warning for the first time
And laughed when I asked him the bewildered question
"What did you do that for?"

It was then that I began laughing myself
And laughed until I felt the pressure in my throat and eyes
Unbearable and laughing I jumped him
With tears streaming down my face I banged his head against the
     wall
And when they pulled me off him I was laughing still
And asking everyone "What did he hit me for?"

I know it is easy to exaggerate
The importance of any event in childhood
I mention the whole thing in (   )
And instead of dwelling on it I will
Continue with some light
Subversive verse
Trying to make despair respectable
And the world safe for remorse.

George Jonas

The Children Are Laughing

It is monday and the children are laughing
The children are laughing; they believe they are princes,
They wear no shoes; they believe they are princes
And their filthy kingdom heaves up behind them

The filthy city heaves up behind them
They are older than I am, their feet are shoeless
They have lived a thousand years; the children are laughing
The children are laughing and their death is upon them

I have cried in the city (the children are laughing)
I have worn many colours (the children are laughing)
They are older than I am, their death is upon them
I will wear no shoes when the princes are dying

Gwendolyn MacEwan

The Dog with a Million Fleas

I heard my mother calling me and groaned, time to get up again. The edges of my window panes sparkled with frost and the sky looked grey, as though it were going to snow. And then I remembered, it was Saturday, the best day of the whole week. I lay there warm and snug and planned what I would do. I know! I would go the the copse. The copse is a name which I gave to the grounds surrounding an old house which has since been pulled down. It is a magic sort of place where one can always find something unusual, there my sister and I have spent many a happy hour wandering about and imagining all sorts of things there. I decided to go to the copse again, and I wondered what I would discover today. The best things always happen to me on a Saturday except Christmas and birthdays as they happen on any day of the week.

I dressed and had my breakfast, mummy made me put on two pairs of socks and then my wellingtons as she said it was going to snow. I put my scarf and gloves on too and pretended I was an explorer in the arctic wastes. I slipped my penknife into my pocket and two russets from the box in the pantry.

Now my penknife is a very special one, and I have never seen another like it, and I feel very proud when people ask to see it, for it has two blades, a corkscrew, a saw, a tin opener, a screwdriver, an awl and even a pair of scissors. My uncle gave it to me for my birthday four years ago.

So I felt very happy as I went down the lane with the penknife and apples in my pocket. I wished I had brought my dog Dandy with me as he loves exploring too, he is not an ordinary dog, everyone else seems to have dogs like poodles, dachshunds and dogs like that, but my dog is a cross-bred terrier, some people say he's only a mongrel, and I tell them he's cleverer than any dog I've ever met, he can play hide and seek and he doesn't cheat either! You can leave him in the potting shed, and tell him to stay and hide his eyes, then hide yourself and whistle him, and he always finds you, he joins in all our games and he is four years old, and we bought him for twelve and six from the Manchester Dogs Home and mummy says he's the best twelve and sixpennyworth she has ever seen. Anyway I must tell you about my visit to the copse when I got there the ground was white with frost and it made everything look different. I didn't see any birds, or anything at all, the copse seemed quiet and deserted but a little dog with a rough curly coat came trotting up to me, it barked at first but when I talked to it a little it wagged its tail and let me pat it, every so often it shook itself, sat down and started to scratch furiously and then I heard a whistle and looked up and saw a boy, he was about nine years old and had a nice friendly sort of face and he smiled at me.

'That's my dog,' he said, 'He's called Ruff.'

I told him I had a dog too. All the time we were talking I was looking at him. He looked very cold as his clothes seemed too small for him, his jacket sleeves were very short and his thin wrists stuck out, and his hands were very red, he kept rubbing them together. He was a thin sort of a boy and very cheerful and I liked him a lot. He said he had never been to the copse before. I showed him my penknife while we were talking and I could see he thought it was marvellous. He kept on opening and shutting the blades and cutting little bits of wood that lay about. And then he said rather sadly, 'I wish I had one like it,' and I said, 'Why don't you ask your father to buy you one for Christmas?' He said very quickly, 'I haven't got a father.' I could tell by the way he spoke he didn't want to say any more, so I offered him an apple. He bit a piece off for his dog and then asked me what made the skins wrinkled like that. 'It's a russet,' I said. 'My father picks them from the trees and puts them by for winter.' 'Have you got your own apple trees,' he said in surprise, 'How many have you got?' I was going to say eight when I stopped. How could I say I had eight apple trees when he hadn't even got a father. 'Oh, we've only got one,' I said, 'and it's not a very good one either.' 'This tastes all right to me,' he said. All the time he had been talking to me, his little dog had been running round and jumping up at him and licking his hands, you could see the dog loved him. And he would bend down and rub the dog's ears and fuss him as if he loved him too and every so often the dog would shake himself violently and scratch himself first one place and then another, it made me tickle all over just to look at him. 'Why does he keep shaking and scratching,' I asked. 'Oh!' he said, 'He can't help it, he's got fleas.' 'Fleas?' I said. 'Yes,' he said proudly. 'He's got about a million of them.' 'Doesn't he mind,' I said. 'Oh, no,' he answered. 'He's always had them.' What with scratching and shaking and jumping and licking he was the funniest little dog I have ever seen. The boy took something from his pocket. 'Look at this,' he said. It was a large marble and it had a lovely coloured whirly line going round inside it. He told me to look through it, and I did so, it looked beautiful and he was very pleased when I told him it was the best one I had ever seen. 'Would you like it?' he said. 'Oh, no, I couldn't take it,' I told him. 'Go on,' he said, 'I want you to have it.' He pressed it in my hand and said, 'I must go now. I'll come again next week.' He whistled his dog who was scratching as though his life depended on it, he bounded after the boy, and off they went, when he came to the trees he turned and waved, and I waved back, I still had the marble in one hand and my penknife in the other, in a moment the boy and the dog had gone.

I stood there feeling very miserable, I had such a lot of things I could easily have given him the knife. He had only had a marble and he had given that to me. I went home and went up to my room to think it over, my dog came with me, I sat on my bed and he pushed his nose into my hands, he knew how I felt, he may not have the fleas but he's very understanding. I put the marble and the penknife in my top drawer and went downstairs. I told mummy all about it and asked her what I should have done, and she asked me what I would do if the same thing should happen all over again and I said that I would give him the knife, so I made up my mind that if he came the next week I would give it to him. Now in nearly all books I have read the stories have happy endings but this one hasn't. Although I went back to the copse many times I didn't see the boy or dog again. It doesn't seem the same magic place any more, the workmen have been and cut down most of the trees and it's just a large space now.

Mummy said when I asked her why, 'Nothing ever stands still, things are changing all the time.'

It all happened a long time ago, but I still have the penknife and marble. I don't suppose I will ever see him again, it used to make me feel unhappy but when I think of the boy now I don't feel sad about him any more. My mother said that anyone with a nice little dog like Ruff couldn't help feeling happy. So I think of him as I last saw him waving to me through the trees with his little dog jumping up and down and running round him, the dog that loved him best in the world, the dog with a million fleas!

Stuart Widdows, aged 12

Children and School

About School

First Day

The teacher sat behind a desk of unpainted wood and when he said good morning he smiled at us and asked our names. Bert told him, his and mine too. By this time, I did not know mine.

He told us we could sit together, until he got the classes all arranged. I was too shy to look around at the strange children but I was surprised to know how many children there were. I wondered where they had all come from. There were fifteen or sixteen.

In front of us sat Annie Adams, dressed in a lovely navy blue cashmere dress, with red piping and brass buttons, and she had two long brown braids with a red ribbon braided in them, and a bow on the nape of her neck and one on the end of each braid. Not only that, but had a circular comb in her hair and a red one at that. I felt naked and ashamed with my round shingled head, destitute of ribbons, or any place to put a ribbon. Annie had every piece of equipment a provident child could think of. The frame of her slate was covered with red felt and her slate rag, a piece of white cotton, had a herringboned hem and a heavy glass salt cellar, filled with water, indicated a source of moisture. She even had a pen wiper.

The teacher was finding out what we knew and looking at the books we brought. When he called me to come up to his desk bringing my books I had nothing to bring but a battered old 'Second-part' Ontario Reader and a slate with nothing on its frame. I could tell of no school experiences at all. 'I cannot read,' I confessed miserably.

He smiled at me again and said, 'Never mind that, you'll soon learn.'

'I am nearly ten,' I said, determined to tell all.

'Good!' he said, 'a very good time to begin school; you'll be reading in three months.' I looked at him then and the compact was sealed. I knew I would be reading in three months. I knew my burden of ignorance was going to be lifted.

Excerpt from *Clearing In The West* by **Nellie McClung**

Village School

The morning came, without any warning, when my sisters surrounded me, wrapped me in scarves, tied up my boot-laces, thrust a cap on my head, and stuffed a baked potato in my pocket.

"What's this?" I said.

"You're starting school today."

"I ain't. I'm stopping 'ome."

"Now, come on, Loll. You're a big boy now."

"I ain't"

"You are."

"Boo-hoo."

They picked me up bodily, kicking and bawling, and carried me up to the road.

"Boys who don't go to school get put into boxes, and turn into rabbits, and get chopped up Sundays."

I felt this was overdoing it rather, but I said no more after that. I arrived at the school just three feet tall and fatly wrapped in my scarves. The playground roared like a rodeo, and the potato burned through my thigh. Old boots, ragged stockings, torn trousers and skirts, went skating and skidding around me. The rabble closed in; I was encircled; grit flew in my face like shrapnel. Tall girls with frizzled hair, and huge boys with sharp elbows, began to prod me with hideous interest. They plucked at my scarves, spun me round like a top, screwed my nose and stole my potato.

I was rescued at last by a gracious lady — the sixteen-year-old junior-teacher — who boxed a few ears and dried my face and led me off to The Infants. I spent that first day picking holes in paper, then went home in a smouldering temper.

"What's the matter, Loll? Didn't he like it at school, then?"

They never gave me the present!"

"Present? What present?"

"They said they'd give me a present."

"Well, now, I'm sure they didn't."

"They did! They said: 'You're Laurie Lee, ain't you? Well, just you sit there for the present.' I sat there all day but I never got it. I ain't going back there again!"

Excerpt from *Cider with Rosie* by **Laurie Lee**

Timothy Winters

Timothy Winters comes to school
With eyes as wide as a football-pool,
Ears like bombs and teeth like splinters:
A blitz of a boy is Timothy Winters.

His belly is white, his neck is dark,
And his hair is an exclamation-mark.
His clothes are enough to scare a crow
And through his britches the blue winds blow.

When teacher talks he won't hear a word
And he shoots down dead the arithmetic-bird,
He licks the patterns off his plate
And he's not even heard of the Welfare State.

Timothy Winters has bloody feet
And he lives in a house on Suez Street
He sleeps in a sack on the kitchen floor
And they say there aren't boys like him any more.

Old Man Winters likes his beer
And his missus ran off with a bombardier,
Grandma sits in the grate with a grin
And Timothy's dosed with an aspirin.

The Welfare Worker lies awake
But the law's as tricky as a ten-foot snake,
So Timothy Winters drinks his cup
And slowly goes on growing up.

At Morning Prayers the Master helves
For children less fortunate than ourselves,
And the loudest response in the room is when
Timothy Winters, roars 'Amen!'

So come one angel, come on ten:
Timothy Winters says 'Amen
Amen amen amen amen.'
Timothy Winters, Lord.
                        Amen.

Charles Causley

Exercise Book

Two and two four
four and four eight
eight and eight sixteen ...
Once again! says the master
Two and two four
four and four eight
eight and eight sixteen.
But look! the lyre-bird
high on the wing
the child sees it
the child hears it
the child calls it
Save me
play with me
bird!
So the bird alights
and plays with the child
Two and two four
Once again! says the master
and the child plays
and the bird plays too ...
Four and four eight
eight and eight sixteen
and twice sixteen makes what?
Twice sixteen makes nothing
least of all thirty-two
anyhow
and off they go.
For the child has hidden
the bird in his desk
and all the children
hear its song
and all the children
hear the music
and eight and eight in their turn
off they go
and four and four and two and two
in their turn fade away
and one and one make neither one nor two
but one by one off they go.
And the lyre-bird sings
and the child sings
and the master shouts
When you've quite finished playing the fool!

But all the children
are listening to the music
and the walls of the classroom
quietly crumble.
The windowpanes turn
once more to sand
the ink is sea
the desk is trees
the chalk is cliffs
and the quill pen
a bird again.

Jacques Prévert
Translated from the French by **Paul Dehn**

Excerpt from **Oliver Twist**

The room in which the boys were fed, was a large stone hall, with a copper at one end: out of which the master, dressed in an apron for the purpose, and assisted by one or two women, ladled the gruel at meal-times. Of the festive compostion each boy had one porringer, and no more — except on occasions of great public rejoicing, when he had two ounces and a quarter of bread besides. The bowls never wanted washing. The boys polished them with their spoons till they shone again; and when they had performed this operation (which never took very long, the spoons being nearly as large as the bowls), they would sit staring at the copper, with such eager eyes, as if they could have devoured the very bricks of which it was composed; employing themselves, meanwhile, in sucking their fingers most assiduously, with the view of catching up any stray splashes of gruel that might have been cast thereon. Boys have generally excellent appetites. Oliver Twist and his companions suffered the tortures of slow starvation for three months: at last they got so voracious and wild with hunger, that one boy, who was tall for his age, and hadn't been used to that sort of thing (for his father had kept a small cook-shop), hinted darkly to his companions, that unless he had another basin of gruel *per diem*, he was afraid he might some night happen to eat the boy who slept next to him, who happened to be a weakly youth of tender age. He had a wild, hungry eye; and they implicitly believed him. A council was held; lots were cast who should walk up to the master after supper that evening, and ask for more; and it fell to Oliver Twist.

The evening arrived; the boys took their places. The master in his cook's uniform, stationed himself at the copper; his pauper assistants ranged themselves behind him; the gruel was served out; and a long grace was said over the short commons. The gruel disappeared; the boys whispered each other, and winked at Oliver; while his next neighbours nudged him. Child as he was, he was desperate with hunger, and reckless with misery. He rose from the table; and advancing to the master, basin and spoon in hand, said; somewhat alarmed at his own temerity:

'Please, sir, I want some more.'

The master was a fat, healthy man; but he turned very pale. He gazed in stupefied astonishment on the small rebel for some seconds, and then clung for support to the copper. The assistants were paralysed with wonder; the boys with fear.

'What!' said the master at length, in a faint voice.

'Please, sir,' replied Oliver, 'I want some more.'

The master aimed a blow at Oliver's head with the ladle; pinioned him in his arms; and shrieked aloud for the beadle.

The board were sitting in solemn conclave, when Mr. Bumble rushed into the room in great excitement, and addressing the gentleman in the high chair, said,

'Mr. Limbkins, I beg your pardon, sir! Oliver Twist has asked for more!'

There was a general start. Horror was depicted on every countenance.

'For *more*!' said Mr. Limbkins. 'Compose yourself, Bumble, and answer me distinctly. Do I understand that he asked for more, after he had eaten the supper allotted by the dietary?'

'He did, sir,' replied Bumble.

'That boy will be hung,' said the gentleman in the white waistcoat. 'I never was more convinced of anything in my life, than I am that that boy will ˥ome to be hung.'

Charles Dickens

A Boy's Head

In it there is a space-ship
and a project
for doing away with piano lessons.

And there is
Noah's ark,
which shall be first.

And there is
an entirely new bird,
an entirely new hare,
an entirely new bumble-bee.

There is a river
that flows upwards.

There is a multiplication table.

There is anti-matter.

And it just cannot be trimmed.

I believe
that only what cannot be trimmed
is a head.

There is much promise
in the circumstance
that so many people have heads.

Miroslav Holub
Translated from the Czech by **Ian Milner**

About School

He always
He always wanted to explain things, but no one cared,
So he drew.

Sometimes he would just draw and it wasn't anything.
He wanted to carve it in stone or write it in the sky.
He would lie out on the grass and look up in the sky and it would
    be only the sky and things inside him that needed saying.

And it was after that that he drew the picture,
It was a beautiful picture. He kept it under his pillow and would
    let no one see it.
And he would look at it every night and think about it.
And when it was dark and his eyes were closed he could see it
    still.
And it was all of him and he loved it.

When he started school he brought it with him,
Not to show anyone, but just to have with him like a friend.

It was funny about school.
He sat in a square brown room, like all the other rooms,
And it was tight and close, and stiff.

He hated to hold the pencil and chalk, with his arm stiff and
    his feet flat on the floor, stiff, with the teacher watching
    and watching.

The teacher came and spoke to him.
She told him to wear a tie like all the other boys,
He said he didn't like them and she said it didn't matter.
After that he drew. And he drew all yellow and it was the way
    he felt about morning. And it was beautiful.

The teacher came and smiled at him. "What's this?" she said.
Why don't you draw something like Ken's drawing?
    Isn't it beautiful?"

After that his mother bought him a tie and he always drew air-
    planes and rocket-ships like everyone else.
And he threw the old picture away.
And when he lay all alone looking at the sky, it was big and blue,
    and all of everything, but he wasn't anymore.

He was square and brown inside and his hands were stiff.
And he was like everyone else. All the things inside him that
    needed saying didn't need it anymore.

It had stopped pushing. It was crushed.
Stiff
Like everything else.
                       Anon

The School Globe

Sometimes when I hold
Our faded old globe
That we used at school
To see where oceans were
And the five continents,
The lines of latitude and longitude,
The North Pole, the Equator and the South Pole —
Sometimes when I hold this
Wrecked blue cardboard pumpkin
I think: here in my hands
Rest the fair fields and lands
Of my childhood
Where still lie or still wander
Old games, tops and pets;
A house where I was little
And afraid to swear
Because God might hear and
Send a bear
To eat me up:
Rooms where I was as old
As I was high;
Where I loved the pink clenches,
The white, red and pink fists
Of roses; where I watched the rain
That Heaven's clouds threw down
In puddles and rutfuls
And irregular mirrors
Of soft brown glass upon the ground.
This school globe is a parcel of my past,
A basket of pluperfect things.
And here I stand with it
Sometime in the summertime
All alone in an empty schoolroom
Where about me hang
Old maps, an abacus, pictures,
Blackboards, empty desks.
If I raise my hand
No tall teacher will demand
What I want.
But if someone in authority
Were here, I'd say
Give me this old world back

Whose husk I clasp
And I'll give you in exchange
The great sad real one
That's filled
Not with a child's remembered and pleasant skies,
But with blood, pus, horror, death, step-mothers, and lies.

James Reaney

Children and Make·believe

I, Icarus

Legend

The blacksmith's boy went out with a rifle
and a black dog running behind.
Cobwebs snatched at his feet,
rivers hindered him,
thorn branches caught at his eyes to make him blind
and the sky turned into an unlucky opal,
but he didn't mind,
I can break branches, I can swim rivers, I can stare out any
     spider I meet,
said he to his dog and his rifle.

The blacksmith's boy went over the paddocks
with his old black hat on his head.
Mountains jumped in his way,
rocks rolled down on him,
and the old crow cried, You'll soon be dead.
And the rain came down like mattocks.
But he only said
I can climb mountains, I can dodge rocks, I can shoot an
     old crow any day.
and he went on over the paddocks.

When he came to the end of the day the sun began falling.
Up came the night ready to swallow him,
like the barrel of a gun,
like an old black hat,
like a black dog hungry to follow him.
Then the pigeon, the magpie, and the dove began wailing
and the grass lay down to billow him.
His rifle broke, his hat flew away and his dog was gone
and the sun was falling.

But in front of the night the rainbow stood on a mountain,
just as his heart foretold.
He ran like a hare,
he climbed like a fox;
he caught it in his hands, the color and the cold —
like a bar of ice, like the column of a fountain,
like a ring of gold.
The pigeon, the magpie, and the dove flew up to stare,
and the grass stood up again on the mountain.

The blacksmith's boy hung the rainbow on his shoulder
instead of his broken gun.
Lizards ran out to see,
snakes made way for him,

and the rainbow shone as brightly as the sun.
All the world said, Nobody is braver, nobody is bolder,
nobody else has done
anything to equal it. He went home as bold as he could be
with the swinging rainbow on his shoulder.

Judith Wright

maggie and milly and molly and may

maggie and milly and molly and may
went down to the beach (to play one day)

and maggie discovered a shell that sang
so sweetly she couldn't remember her troubles, and

milly befriended a stranded star
whose rays five languid fingers were;

and molly was chased by a horrible thing
which raced sideways while blowing bubbles: and

may came home with a smooth round stone
as small as a world and as large as alone.

For whatever we lose (like a you or a me)
it's always ourselves we find in the sea

e.e. cummings

Excerpt from *Portrait of the Artist as a Young Dog*

Gwilym's chapel was the last old barn before the field that led down to the river; it stood well above the farm-yard, on a mucky hill. There was one whole door with a heavy padlock, but you could get in easily through the holes on either side of it. He took out a ring of keys and shook them gently and tried each one in the lock. 'Very posh,' he said; 'I bought them from the junk-shop in Carmarthen.' We climbed into the chapel through a hole.

A dusty wagon with the name painted out and a whitewash cross on its side stood in the middle. 'My pulpit cart,' he said, and walked solemnly into it up the broken shaft. 'You sit on the hay; mind the mice,' he said. Then he brought out his deepest voice again, and cried to the heavens and the bat-lined rafters and the hanging webs: 'Bless us this holy day, O Lord, bless me and Dylan and this Thy little chapel for ever and ever, Amen. I've done a lot of improvements to this place.'

I sat on the hay and stared at Gwilym preaching, and heard his voice rise and crack and sink to a whisper and break into singing and Welsh and ring triumphantly and be wild and meek. The sun, through a hole, shone on his praying shoulders, and he said: 'O God, Thou art everywhere all the time, in the dew of the morning, in the frost of the evening, in the field and the town, in the preacher and the sinner, in the sparrow and the big buzzard. Thou canst see everything, right down deep in our hearts; Thou canst see us when the sun is gone; Thou canst see us when there aren't any stars, in the gravy blackness, in the deep, deep, deep, deep pit; Thou canst see and spy and watch us all the time, in the little black corners, in the big cowboys' prairies, under the blankets when we're snoring fast, in the terrible shadows, pitch black, pitch black; Thou canst see everything we do, in the night and the day, in the day and the night, everything, everything; Thou canst see all the time. O God, mun, you're like a cat.'

He let his clasped hands fall. The chapel in the barn was still, and shafted with sunlight. There was nobody to cry Hallelujah or God-bless; I was too small and enamoured in the silence. The one duck quacked outside.

'Now I take a collection,' Gwilym said.

He stepped down from the cart and groped about in the hay beneath it and held out a battered tin to me.

'I haven't got a proper box,' he said.

I put two pennies in the tin.

'It's time for dinner,' he said, and we went back to the house without a word.

Dylan Thomas

I, Icarus

There was a time when I could fly, I swear it.
Perhaps, if I think hard for a moment, I can even tell you the year.
My room was on the ground floor at the rear of the house.
My bed faced a window.
Night after night I lay on my bed and willed myself to fly.
It was hard work, I can tell you.
Sometimes I lay perfectly still for an hour before I felt
    my body rising from the bed.
I rose slowly, slowly until I floated three or four feet
    above the floor.
Then, with a kind of swimming motion, I propelled myself
    toward the window.
Outside, I rose higher and higher, above the pasture fence,
    above the clothesline, above the dark, haunted trees
    beyond the pasture.
And, all the time, I heard the music of flutes.
It seemed the wind made this music.
And sometimes there were voices singing.

Alden Nowlan

And What If

And what if he looks
silly? A child
on a wooden horse.

And what if he has
shut his eyes? A race
with only one entry.

And what if he is
lost? The reins
over the rump

I wish him joy
and a turbulent ride.

Gael Turnbull

A Backwards Journey

When I was a child of say, seven
I still had serious attention to give
to everyday objects. The Dutch Cleanser —
which was the kind my mother bought —
in those days came in a round container
of yellow cardboard around which ran
the very busy Dutch Cleanser woman
her face hidden behind her bonnet
holding a yellow Dutch Cleanser can
on which a smaller Dutch Cleanser woman
was holding a smaller Dutch Cleanser can
on which a minute Dutch Cleanser woman
held an imagined Dutch Cleanser can ....

This was no game. The woman led me
backwards through the eye of the mind
until she was the smallest point
my thought could hold to. And at that moment
I think I knew that if no one called
and nothing broke the delicate jet
of my attention, that tiny image
could smash the atom of space and time.

P.K. Page

The Unicorn

Intended to be spoken at the opening of the
Unicorn Theatre for Children

Who can tell me in what kingdom
Roams the wild, white Unicorn?
In all countries you may find him,
At all hours he is born.

Will I need a woven halter
For a beast so swift and rare?
Empty-handed you must find him
Where he hovers in the air.

Who can tell me when to seek him?
Who can tell me when to rest?
He is kind to all who call him,
And he loves the youngest best.

If I find him, can I hold him?
Will he vanish like the day?
Once you turn your eyes upon him,
He will never go away.

Books are brief, and pictures faded.
Tell me then what I shall find.
Wild and white and smooth as water
He will shiver in your mind.

Will he not grow tame and common
If I touch him with my hand?
He is yours, yet he is never
Less than free in every land.

Show me then how I must seek him,
Tell me then when I must leave.
But the quest is made of magic:
You have only to believe.

Mary Oliver

Children and Relatives

The Night Grandma Died

Roots

I've seen only one picture of my great-grandfather.
He was pointed out to me
as the fourth man from the left in a photograph
of about thirty men and two teams of horses
posed in front of a logging camp in the 1880's.
You find the same kind of picture
in histories of the west, a posse
come back with the bodies, they used to prop up the dead
with their eyes still open and pretend
to be holding them at gunpoint.
                              And I seem to remember
similar pictures of the Serbian army
during the First World War, my great-grandfather
even wore a sort of Slavic blouse
and the same kind of moustache.
                              There are also pictures
of white men after a lynching.
                              Nobody is smiling
because these were time-exposures
and if you must keep your face still
it's safest and simplest
to shut your mouth, although best
not to clench your teeth because then
you may start to imagine
you're smothering, take a deep breath
and spoil everything,
and their eyes are black slits
because it's impossible
to keep from blinking once you try not to.
Though I don't believe they'd have smiled
even if that had been mechanically possible.
It was a ritual then, this picture-taking,
the photographer down from Halifax,
a city man in a linen collar and a derby hat,
who put a black hood over his head and sometimes
set off an explosion at the crucial moment
They knew
this was an instant
that could be held
against them.
So they look very tough and their hands are free
or grip peaveys or axes.
                              I get the feeling
my great-grandfather is trying to convince somebody

64

he'd use that axe on a man, if he had to.
He holds it the way those Serbs held their rifles.
And I have no doubt.
he'd have joined a manhunt
or helped with a lynching,
would have thought it unmanly
to have done otherwise.
                        Or maybe it's only
that he's proud of the axe,
maybe he was an axeman like his grandson, my father,
who could make the tallest tree
fall where he wanted it, aim its tip at a spot
no bigger than a fig
of chewing tobacco, and hit it.
I read the histories of countries
and his time seems like yesterday
but because he was human
and my own, he seems so old
as to almost stand
outside of time.
                    It amazes me, thinking:
he must have been at least fifteen years
younger than I am that day the winter sun
lapped up and locked into a small black box
an infinitesimal portion of his soul.

Alden Nowlan

The Night Grandma Died

"Here's Grandmother in here," Cousin Joy said,
Standing beside me at the bedroom door,
One hand on my shoulder. "You see, she's only sleeping."
But I, nine years old and frightened,
Knew it was a lie, Grandmother's shell
Lay on the bed, hands folded, head on one side,
The spirit that had groaned so loud an hour ago
Gone out of her. I looked, and turned and ran,
First to the kitchen. There were the aunts
Who had laid her out, still weeping
Over a good hot cup of tea: Aunt Stella,
Large, dominant; Aunt Alice, a plump, ruffled hen of a woman;
My small, quick mother; Aunt Grace, youngest and shyest,
Awkward on the edge of the group: "Shush," she was saying
To Cousin Pauline, who was lying on the floor
Pretending to be Grandma.

And they all got up and came into the parlour,
Where suddenly everyone was jovial,
And Aunt April sat in the best chair
Nursing her newest baby,
And the uncles sat talking of crops and weather,
And Uncle Harry, who had come from Maine,
Pumped the hands of people he hadn't seen in twenty years,
And Grandma's nephew Eb from up the road
Played everybody's favourite tune on the piano.
Now and then, remembering the corpse, he burst into a Baptist hymn,
His rich bass voice, dark and deep as molasses,
Flowing protectively over the women,
While his eyes, also dark,
Wrapped them warm with sympathy.

And I, sitting on a footstool in a corner,
Was sometimes warmed by the voice,
And sometimes chilled remembering
In the room next door
Grandmother, dead, whom I had never liked.

Elizabeth Brewster

The Bratty Brother (Sister)

I dumped the bratty brother
in a shark-infested sea;
By dusk the sea was empty, and
The brat was home with me.

I mailed the bratty brother
To a jail in Moosonee,
The sobbing jailer mailed him back
The next day, C.O.D.

I wept, and hurled the bratty
Brother off the CN Tower;
He lolloped through the living room
In less than half an hour.

So now I keep my brother
In the furnace, nice and neat.
I can't wait till December
When my Dad turns on the heat.

Dennis Lee

A Grandfather

When I visited my grandfather
                              as a child
he was constantly mending
pouncing on buttonless pants
cradling toeless socks
sewing up sails
it was the sails that fascinated me
and watching him by the hour
welding old canvas into mythical voyages
I asked to come along
though the rain fell continuously on our plans
and his old boat rotted like a wooden tombstone
                    in the backyard
his hands   deftly melting needle and twine
into yielding oceans
were awkward with grandchildren
looking up from his sewing

67

he'd grope frantically for names
exorcising evil spirits
by patting assorted unrecognized heads
and seeing that we did not stir
flounder in his pockets
for pennies

I stood around
until my teens
when the whole notion of a voyage sank
The ever-present patches
oulined like neon signs on his pants
affronted me
and indignant
I reflected on the snow white grandfathers
who withered away beautifully
in the movies
and knew my presence now was part of a continual apology.

and when he lay
more stranger to himself that to his family
on an unfamiliar bed
I saw my mother holding out her hands to him
and putting together the pieces of my life
wondered what new rights imminent death had given me
and if it were too early   or too late
           to introduce myself
                     again
                          to this old man.

Florence McNeil

Grandfather

Grandfather
        Jabez Harry Bowering
strode across the Canadian prairie
hacking down trees
               & building churches
delivering personal baptist sermons in them
leading Holy holy holy lord god almighty songs in them
red haired man squared off in the pulpit
reading Saul on the road to Damascus at them

Left home
        big walled Bristol town
at age eight
        to make a living
buried his stubby fingers in root snarled earth
for a suit of clothes & seven hundred gruelly meals a year
taking an anabaptist cane across the back every day
for four years till he was whipt out of England

Twelve years old
           & across the ocean alone
to apocalyptic Canada
           Ontario of bone bending labor
six years on the road to Damascus till his eyes were blinded
with the blast of Christ & he wandered west
to Brandon among wheat kings & heathen Saturday nights
young red haired Bristol boy shoveling coal
in the basement of Brandon college five in the morning

Then built his first wooden church & married
a sick girl who bore two live children & died
leaving several pitiful letters & the Manitoba night

He moved west with another wife & built children & churches
Saskatchewan Alberta British Columbia Holy holy holy
lord god almighty
        struck his labored bones with pain
& left him a postmaster prodding grandchildren with crutches
another dead wife & a glass bowl of photographs
& holy books unopened save the bible by the bed

Till he died the day before his eighty-fifth birthday
in a Catholic hospital of sheets white as his hair

George Bowering

Children at Christmas

Who Has Seen The Wind

Excerpt from **Cameos of Pioneer Life in Western Canada**

Preparations for the great day started as soon as evenings grew dark and cold early and the little children of the house could be sent to bed in time to give the older members a chance to do sewing without being seen and questioned. Our nearest store was 165 miles away and buying was entirely out of the question. There was no mail service and would be none till spring so if there was to be any toys or games they must be made by hand. With both tools and material being scarce my sister and I resorted to the rag bag, for, as she said 'We just have to have Christmas and the little girls must have dolls without suspecting anything about them. The best of it is the surprise.' Mother gave us leave and we two girls clipped and sewed the pretty pieces from the rag bag till we had fashioned three good dolls, one blue, one red and one red plaid, every whit hand-made out of rags. Even the heads were of white cotton with eyes, nose, mouth, etc. sewed in black cotton thread.

Father and mother planned to surprise us also. I think it could not be easily done when the whole family lives in a 12 by 24 sod shanty with only curtain partitions. Of course we all hung up our stockings on Christmas Eve, just for fun. My elder sister had told me about the dear old myth, as she called it, and that I was old enough to know the truth and we must not be disappointed because we did not get anything. So we all wakened very early in the cold frosty darkness and felt around for our stockings just to pretend, but were surprised to find real surprises. In each of our stockings were a little parcel of real raisins and three cookies. We two oldest girls had very pretty little gold brooches and the three younger ones their dolls. Beautiful? Of course they thought so and mother said they were much better than boughten ones for they would not break.

When we had eaten our cookies and raisins and emphatically decided we were having a very happy Christmas we cuddled down again until our teeth stopped chattering. Then we all got up, lit the fire and got breakfast as a Christmas present to our parents and they very obligingly stayed asleep till we were ready. After breakfast, dishes washed, floor swept and general chores done, the sun came out nice and bright and we went for a sleigh ride with the white oxen, Brisk and Lively, while mother stayed home and prepared dinner. Oh what a dinner! Roasted prairie chicken with dressing and gravy, potatoes mashed with butter in plenty and such a pudding boiled in a cloth, with real raisins and butter instead of suet (suet had been sent for in November but did not arrive until February), dried Saskatoon berries instead of currants and several other substitutes but the pudding was real good. We had a lovely drive and got back as hungry as hunters, so it was all good.

After dinner, the first meal on a real table in the West (father had finished making the table on Christmas day in the forenoon) we washed dishes and cleared up a little and it was evening already. We sat around the blazing wood fire and mother sang to us for some time. Then father told us several stories, or rather one story from several viewpoints. In our minds there is still the firelight picture and the remembrance of the story of the shepherds watching their flocks by night, of the wise men with their gifts so valuable, of the wicked King Herod who was so jealous of his poor kingdom and the dear little Babe in the manger. That first Christmas! Although some may think we were then in a wilderness, and truly it was, but not God forsaken, no we thought it almost Heaven.

Kate Johnson

Parade Of The Toys

Every street crowded with children
going downtown to see Santa Claus
and all twelve prancing reindeer
drawn through the streets of Toronto.

Drink it all in, little eyes,
little ears, little hearts,
believe in it as you've never
believed anything before.

Because it won't last very long —
before you know it they'll shatter
every dream you ever had,
and there won't be Santa anymore

but only windows piled with junk,
happy drunks at every corner,
and the people crying like children
at a world they don't know anymore.

Raymond Souster

Excerpt from **A Child's Christmas In Wales**

It was on the afternoon of the day
of Christmas Eve, and I was in Mrs. Prothero's
garden, waiting for cats, with her son Jim,
It was snowing. It was always snowing at Christmas.
December, in my memory, is white as Lapland,
though there were no reindeers.
But there were cats. Patient, cold and callous,
our hands wrapped in socks, we waited
to snowball the cats. Sleek and long as jaguars
and horrible-whiskered, spitting and snarling,
they would slink and sidle over the white
back-garden walls, and the lynx-eyed hunters,
Jim and I, fur-capped and moccasined trappers
from Hudson Bay, off Mumbles Road, would hurl
our deadly snowballs at the green of their eyes.

The wise cats never appeared. We were so still
Eskimo-footed arctic marksmen in the muffling
silence of the eternal snows - eternal,
ever since Wednesday — that we never heard
Mrs. Prothero's first cry for her igloo at the
bottom of the garden. Or, if we heard it at all,
it was, to us, like the far-off challenge of our enemy
and prey, the neighbour's polar cat. But soon
the voice grew louder. 'Fire!' cried Mrs. Prothero,
and she beat the dinner-gong.

And we ran down the garden, with the snowballs
in our arms, toward the house;and smoke,
indeed, was pouring out of the dining-room,
and the gong was bombilating, and Mrs. Prothero
was announcing ruin like a town crier in Pompeii.
This was better than all the cats in Wales
standing on the wall in a row. We bounded into
the house, laden with snowballs, and stopped at
the open door of the smoke-filled room.

Something was burning all right;
perhaps it was Mr. Prothero, who always slept
there after midday dinner with a newspaper
over his face. But he was standing in the middle
of the room, saying, 'A fine Christmas!'
and smacking at the smoke with a slipper.
'Call the fire brigade,' cried Mrs. Prothero
as she beat the gong.

'They won't be there,' said Mr. Prothero,
'it's Christmas.'

There was no fire to be seen, only clouds of smoke
and Mr. Prothero standing in the middle of them,
waving his slipper as though he were conducting.

'Do something,' he said.
And we threw all our snowballs into the smoke —
I think we missed Mr. Prothero — and ran out
of the house to the telephone box.

'Let's call the police as well,' Jim said.

'And the ambulance.'

'And Ernie Jenkins, he likes fires.'

But we only called the fire brigade, and soon
the fire engine came and three tall men in helmets
brought a hose into the house and Mr. Prothero
got out just in time before they turned it on.
Nobody could have had a noisier Christmas Eve.
And when the firemen turned off the hose and
were standing in the wet, smoky room, Jim's aunt,
Miss Prothero, came downstairs and peered in
at them. Jim and I waited, very quietly, to hear what
she would say to them. She said the right thing,
always. She looked at the three tall firemen in their
shining helmets, standing among the smoke and
cinders and dissolving snowballs, and she said:
"Would you like anything to read?"

Dylan Thomas

Excerpt from **Act One**

It was the Christmas after my aunt had left the house, and since it was she who always supplied the tree and the presents for my brother and myself, this first Christmas without her was a bleak and empty one. I remember that I was more or less reconciled to it, because my father had worked only spasmodically throughout the year. Two of our rooms were vacant of boarders and my mother was doing her marketing farther and farther away from our neighbourhood. This was always a sign that we were dangerously close to rock bottom, and each time it occurred I came to dread it more. It was one of the vicious landmarks of poverty that I had come to know well and the one I hated the most. As the bills at our regular grocer and butcher went unpaid, and my mother dared not even be seen at the stores lest they come to the doorways and yell after her publicly, she would trudge ten or twelve blocks to a whole new neighborhood, tell the new grocer or butcher that we had just moved in to some fictitious address around the corner, and establish credit for as long as she could. Thus we were able to exist until my father found work again, or all the rooms were rented, and she could pay our own grocer and butcher, and gradually the others. This time, however, they had all of them gone unpaid and my mother was walking twenty blocks or more for a bottle of milk.

Obviously Christmas was out of the question — we were barely staying alive. On Christmas Eve my father was very silent during the evening meal. Then he surprised and startled me by turning to me and saying, "Let's take a walk." He had never suggested such a thing before, and moreover it was a very cold winter's night. I was even more surprised when he said as we left the house, "Let's go down to a Hundred Forty-ninth Street and Westchester Avenue." My heart leapt within me. That was the section where all the big stores were, where at Christmastime open pushcarts full of toys stood packed end-to-end for blocks at a stretch. On other Christmas Eves I had often gone there with my aunt, and from our tour of the carts she had gathered what I wanted the most. My father had known of this, of course, and I joyously concluded that this walk could mean only one thing—he was going to buy me a Christmas present.

On the walk down I was beside myself with delight and an inner relief. It had been a bad year for me, that year of my aunt's going, and I wanted a Christmas present terribly — not a present merely, but a symbol, a token of some sort. I needed some sign from my father and mother that they knew what I was going through and cared for me as much as my aunt, and my grandfather did. I am sure they were giving me what mute signs they could, but I did not see them. The idea that my father had managed a Christmas present for me in spite of everything filled me with a sudden peace and lightness of heart I had not known in months.

We hurried on, our heads bent against the wind, to the cluster of lights ahead that was 149th Street and Westchester Avenue, and those lights seemed to me the brightest lights I had ever seen. Tugging at my father's coat, I started down the line of pushcarts. There were all kinds of things that I wanted, but since nothing had been said by my father about buying a present, I would merely pause before a pushcart to say, with as much control as I could muster, "Look at that chemistry set!" or, "There's a stamp album!" or, "Look at the printing press!" Each time my father would pause ask the pushcart man the price. Then without a word we would move on to the next pushcart. Once or twice he would pick up a toy of some kind and look at it and then at me, as if to suggest this might be something I might like, but I was ten years old and a good deal beyond just a toy; my heart was set on a chemistry set or a printing press. There they were on every pushcart we stopped at, but the price was always the same and soon I looked up and saw we were nearing the end of the line. Only two or three more pushcarts remained. My father looked up, too, and I heard him jingle some coins in his pocket. In a flash I knew it all. He'd gotten together about seventy-five cents to buy me a Christmas present, and he hadn't dared say so in case there was nothing to be had for so small a sum.

As I looked up at him I saw a look of despair and disappointment in his eyes that brought me closer to him than I had ever been in my life. I wanted to throw my arms around him and say, "It doesn't matter ... I understand ... this is better than a chemistry set or a printing press ... I love you." But instead we stood shivering beside each other for a moment — then turned away from the last two pushcarts and started silently back home. I don't know why the words remained choked up within me. I didn't even take his hand on the way home nor did he take mine. We were not on that basis. Nor did I ever tell him how close to him I felt that night — that for a little while the concrete wall between father and son had crumbled away and I knew that we were two lonely people struggling to reach each other.

I came close to telling him many years later, but again the moment passed. Again it was Christmas and I was on my way to visit him in Florida. My father was a bright and blooming ninety-one years of age now and I arrived in Florida with my wife to spend Christmas and New Year's with him. On Christmas Eve we sat in his living room, and while my wife chatted with his nurse and companion, I sat on a sofa across the room with my father, showing him the pictures of his two grandchildren. Suddenly I felt his hand slip into mine. It was the first time in our lives that either of us had ever touched the other. No words were spoken and I went right on turning the pages of the picture album, but my hand remained over his. A few years before I might have withdrawn mine after a moment or two, but now my hand remained; nor did I tell him what I was thinking and feeling. The moment was enough. It had taken forty years for the gulf that separated us to close.

Moss Hart

Excerpt from **Who Has Seen the Wind**

In the O'Connal family, Christmas began as a rule early in December, when the boys started to decide what presents they would like. In Brian's second year of school, Christmas was called earlier to the parents' attention because with the beginning of winter Brian asked for skates.

Maggie's first response was unbelief; it was difficult for her to think that one of her boys was old enough to want skates. She reminded him that he was just passed seven and that Forbsie Hoffman did not have skates yet. Brian replied that Art Sherry had them. Art, who was a year and a half older than Brian, had inherited a pair from an older sister; their high tops had been cut down; they had to be worn with three pairs of woolen socks so that Art's feet would not slide around in the shoes — but to Brian, skateless, they were things whose beauty would endure forever.

Skates became a frequent topic of conversation at meals. At length the grandmother said she was sick of hearing about them; would it not be possible to get the child a pair so that he could break his neck and give them a few peaceful meals? Maggie forbade Brian to mention skates at the table again.

The day that he saw the new tube skates in the hardware store window, Brian called on his father at work.

"Why can't I have them, Dad?"

"Because your mother says you're too young for them."

"But I'm not — I'm —"

"Seven's pretty young for skates."

"I was seven a long time ago — in the fall — I'm past seven!"

"You're still too young — when you're older — next year, perhaps."

"I'll be older at Christmas. That's a long ways away. May I have them for Christmas?"

"I don't think so, Spalpeen."

After Brian had left, Gerald felt a pang of remorse; it was difficult to see why the boy could not have skates. That night he had a talk with Maggie.

"Perhaps by Christmas time?" he asked her. "He'll be almost seven and a half then."

His wife looked at him a long time before answering him. "You know — I love him too, Gerald. I hate to deny them things as much as you. It's just that he seems so — do you think he's old enough? Do you — honestly?"

"I think so, Maggie."

"It isn't because he wants them so badly?"

"Well — he's old enough — let him skate."

After a decent interval Brian was told that he might possibly get skates for Christmas. Bobbie then insisted that he should get skates too, but he finally settled for a hockey stick and puck.

Brian looked forward with eagerness to the promised skates. He thought of them often—during school hours—whenever the boys gathered after school with worn, sliver-thin sticks to play a sort of hockey between tin-can goal posts and with a blob of frozen horse manure for a puck. The more he thought of them, the less envious he was of Art with his "wimmen skates." There would be nothing feminine about *his*; they would be sturdy tubes with thick, felt tongues.

The night before Christmas he was almost sick with excitement and anticipation as he lay in his bed with Bobbie beside him. He could see the skates clearly with their frosted tubing and the clear runners that would cling to his thumb when he ran it along them to test their sharpness. He could see himself gliding over the river, alone on shining ice. With a twist and a lean — a shower of ice-snow — he came to a breathtaking stop.

Bobbie stirred in his sleep.

"You awake, Bobbie?"

Bobbie did not answer him.

Perhaps there would be straps over the ankles; not that he would need them, for his ankles were strong. His feet wouldn't slop. He flexed them beneath the covers — stronger than anything. Maybe they were too strong, and when he pushed, he would push the ice clean full of cracks.

He closed his eyes tightly. If only he could get to sleep the time would pass more quickly. When one slept it was nothing — swift as a person on skates — swift as the wind ...

"He came, Brian! He came!"

Bobbie was jumping on the bed, his hair bright in the winter sunshine that filled the room.

Brian jumped from bed, "C'mon!"

Their stockings, lumpy with oranges, each with a colored cardboard clown protruding from its top, hung from the mantel of the fireplace. Bobbie's sleigh that could be steered was before the tree. Bobbie threw himself upon the parcels.

"Wait a minute!" cried Brian. "They're not all yours — just with your name!"

He began to sort out the presents upon which Maggie the night before had printed in the large block letters that Brian could easily read.

Anxiously Brian watched the growing pile of parcels beside him. He opened a deep box to find it full of colored cars and an engine, in little compartments. He opened another — a mechanical affair which when wound caused two long black men to dance, all the while turning around. Slippers were in one promising-looking parcel. As he opened the last of his parcels he was filled with the horrible conviction that something was wrong.

Then he saw a parcel behind the Christmas tree. His name was on it. He opened it. They were not tube scates; they were not single-runnered skates; they were bob-skates, double-runnered affairs with curving toe-cleats and a half-bucket arrangement to catch the heel of the shoe.

For a swift moment Brian's heart was filled with mixed feeling; disappointment bitter and blinding was there, but with it a half-dazed feeling of inner release and relief that he had got the skates. They were skates, he told himself as he turned them over in his hands.

"What's the matter, Brian?" Bobbie had looked up from his fire engine.

Brian got up and went into the living room; he sat on the window seat next to the shamrock plant, the bob-skates upon his knees. When Bobbie came through a while later clutching a hockey stick a foot longer than himself, Brian paid no attention to him.

Throughout dinner he spoke only when spoken to. When his father and uncle were seated in the living room with lighted cigars and his mother and grandmother were in the kitchen, washing the dinner dishes, he went unnoticed to the hallway, put on his coat and toque, and with the bob-skates went out.

He passed other children as he walked, pulling Christmas sleighs and Christmas toboggans, some with gleaming Christmas skates slung over their shoulders. Through the fiercely tinseled snow sparkling unbearably in the sunlight he walked, not toward the downtown bridge where children and adults swooped over cleared ice, but toward the powerhouse and the small footbridge. There he sat near a clump of willow, fitted the skates to his feet, buckled the straps over his insteps, and went knee-deep through the snow on the riverbank to the ice.

Once on the ice he stood for a moment on trembling legs. He pushed with one foot; it skidded sideways; the other went suddenly from under him, and he came down with a bump that snatched his breath. He got carefully up and stood uncertainly. He pushed a tentative skate ahead, then another. He stood still with knees half-bent. He gave a push with one skate preparatory to swooping over the ice. He fell flat on his face. He got up.

He began a slow forward sliding across the ice — painfully — noncommittal steps of a stroke victim just risen from bed. He was not skating, he was walking with an overwhelming feeling of frustration that reminded him of dreams in which he ran with all his might, but stayed only in one spot. He fell again, and felt his elbow go numb. He sat on the ice, looking at his own feet ahead of him.

He began to cry.

Brian's parents, his grandmother, and his uncle were seated in the living room when he got back to the house. He was carrying the bob-skates as he came out of the hallway.

"Been skatin'?" asked Sean.

Brian did not answer him. "Uncle Sean asked you a question, Son," said Maggie.

Sean's big, freckled hand reached out to take one of the bob-skates. "Damn fool question," said Sean. "Fella doesn't skate with bob-skates. Had somebody pullin'you, did you?"

Brain shook his head.

"What's wrong, Spalpeen?" Brian's father was looking at his tear-stained face.

Brian rushed from the room.

"What do you mean?" Maggie turned to Sean. "What's wrong with his skates? What did you mean — "

"They call'em skates," said Sean. "Can't skate with'em. Just teaches kids a healthy respect fer ice, that's all. Got no grip at all — skid like hell. Never forget the first time I took Gerald on ice with a pair — 'bout the same age as Brian. He had one hell of a time — ended up hangin' onto me coattails whilst I pulled him around."

"But — then that means that Brian — he's — " Maggie got up and went swiftly from the room.

She found Brian at the kitchen window.

"Don't they work, Son?"

Still looking out the window, Brian shook his head.

"Aren't they what you wanted?"

"Tubes," he got out with difficulty. "Like in Harris's."

"I'm sorry, Brian." Maggie watched his shoulders moving. She turned his face around to her. "Don't — please don't! I'll fix it!"

She went to the phone.

"Mr. Harris? Have you a pair of — of tube skates left? Small size? I wonder if we — if you could come down to the store with me — my son — will you — will — "

"Mother!"

That night Maggie O'Connal stood at her children's bedside. With her white nightgown almost to her heels, her hair in two black braids, she looked like a little girl in the dimness of the room.

A glinting caught her eye, and she saw a length of leather lace hanging down the side of the bed. Brian slept with his hand clenched around the runner of one tube skate, his nose almost inside the boot. Maggie reached out one hand and laid it lightly upon Brian's cheek; she kept it there for a long time. Then she gently took the skate from his hand.

She turned and with the flat, soft steps of the barefooted went from the room.

W.O. Mitchell

Advice for Children

First Lesson

Enfant

child
listen to father and mother
child
listen to brother and sister
child
cry not
break not
child
shout not
it's not nice
listen to what they say
listen to them they say
child
no one listens to you
it's best that way

Jacques Godbout
Translated from the French by ***John Robert Colombo***

Report

CHORUS: He seems to have the wrong attitude towards Authority
SOLO: Or has Authority the wrong attitude towards him?
CHORUS: He is sprouting in a direction opposite to ours,
How dare he?
How dare this impudent boy dare to question?
Cut him down to size
Quickly.
Twist and warp this growth in our direction.
Mould him
Cast him
If we don't cut him down the world soon will.

If we don't cut him down the world soon will;
This is our justification.
Idealism is wonderful providing it's just words.
And so we'll prune him a little
Because if we don't the world soon will
With this we calm our conscience and our soul.

CHORUS: She will never pass an examination if she continues to waste
her time in this manner.

SOLO: But perhaps she'd be wasting her time trying to
Pass
An examination
CHORUS: There must be some sort of standard
Otherwise how would we spot the passes and the
Failures?
We must sort out the passes and the
Failures.
They must be shown how
Lazy
Idle
And worthless
They are compared with us.
Of course examinations are,
We realize
Bad.
But we are caught in the net of the system;
It's the fault of the system
We all agree.
We often discuss it.
But it's not our fault
We'd change it if we could.
But we'd be voices crying in the wilderness
And the wilderness is lonely.
So we continue to sort out the passes
And the failures.

CHORUS: Seldom pays attention to what is being said in the classroom.
SOLO: Could this be because what is being said is uninteresting and of
little worth to him?
CHORUS: But we are interesting people
We never say worthless things
Because,
You see,
We are teachers.
And Teachers must be listened to
And paid attention to
At all costs.
We were trained for three whole years:
We are qualified.
Therefore we are Oracles
And the children must worship at our shrine.
If they don't we lose our self-respect
And we respect ourselves an awful lot.
We build characters and develop personalities

We are very interesting people
And could never say a worthless thing.

CHORUS: Steady average worker.
SOLO: What does this mean, for God's sake?
CHORUS: It means he sits, and is not a nuisance.
He does not talk unless he is asked to,
He is one of the crowd.
We do not know him very well
Unfortunately.
He is not very good at anything
And yet he is not bad.
He merges into an anonymous mist
When his report confronts us;
We know the whites, and like them
We know the blacks, and hate them
But the greys are
Difficult.
But we must not confess our ignorance,
We must put something down
That is what we are paid and trained for
The classes are too large you see
The system is at fault
We often complain about it
But we dare not do anything
For that would endanger our position.
You have heard the reasons for our weakness
You realize, of course, how much we would do
Were we able.
We would all be better with more pay;
Once a substantial rise comes through
We will be better.
Stronger.
Money is, you see, important.
Other, more menial jobs are at the moment
Worth more than ours
And this is morally wrong.
The dignity of our profession is at stake
And this is most important
More important, at the moment that the children.
Once a substantial rise comes through
Then we will be better.

Anon

First Lesson

The thing to remember about father is, they're men.
A girl has to keep it in mind.
They are dragon-seekers, bent on improbable rescues.
Scratch any father, you find
Someone chock-full of qualms and romantic terrors,
Believing change is a threat —
Like your first shoes with heels on, like your first bicycle
It took such months to get.

Walk in strange woods, they warn you about the snakes there.
Climb, and they fear you'll fall.
Books, angular boys, or swimming in deep water —
Fathers mistrust them all.
Men are the worriers: it is difficult for them
To learn what they must learn:
How you have a journey to take and very likely,
For a while, will not return.

Phyllis McGinley

Matilda

Who told Lies, and was Burned to Death

Matilda told such Dreadful Lies,
It made one Gasp and Stretch one's Eyes;
Her Aunt, who, from her Earliest Youth,
Had kept a Strict Regard for Truth,
Attempted to Believe Matilda:
The effort very nearly killed her,
And would have done so, had not She
Discovered this Infirmity.
For once, towards the Close of Day,
Matilda, growing tired of play,
And finding she was left alone,
Went tiptoe to the Telephone
And summoned the Immediate Aid
Of London's Noble Fire-Brigade.
Within an hour the Gallant Band
Were pouring in on every hand,

From Putney, Hackney Downs and Bow,
With Courage high and Hearts a-glow
They galloped, roaring through the Town,
'Matilda's House is Burning Down!'
Inspired by British Cheers and Loud
Proceeding from the Frenzied Crowd,
They ran their ladders through a score
Of windows on the Ball Room Floor;
And took Peculiar Pains to Souse
The Pictures up and down the House,
Until Matilda's Aunt succeeded
In showing them they were not needed
And even then she had to pay
To get the Men to go away!

.   .   .   .

It happened that a few Weeks later
Her Aunt was off to the Theatre
To see that Interesting Play
The Second Mrs. Tanqueray.
She had refused to take her Niece
To hear this Entertaining Piece:
A Deprivation Just and Wise
To Punish her for Telling Lies.
That Night a Fire *did* break out —
You should have heard Matilda Shout!
You should have heard her Scream and Bawl,
And throw the window up and call
To People passing in the Street —
(The rapidly increasing Heat
Encouraging her to obtain
Their confidence) — but all in vain!
For every time She shouted 'Fire!'
They only answered 'Little Liar!'
And therefore when her Aunt returned,
Matilda, and the House, were Burned.

Hilaire Belloc

Advice To The Young

1
Keep bees and
grow asparagus,
watch the tides
and listen to the
wind instead of
the politicians
make up our own
stories and believe
them if you want to
live the good life.

2
All rituals
are instincts
never fully
trust them
study them
study to im-
prove biology
with reason.

3
Digging trenches
for asparagus
is good for the
muscles and
waiting for the
plants to settle
teaches patience
to those who are
usually in too
much of a hurry.

4
There is morality
in bee-keeping
it teaches how
not to be afraid
of the bee swarm
it teaches how
not to be afraid of
finding new places
and building them
all over again.

Miriam Waddington

89

Child Love

An Ounce of Cure

An Ounce of Cure

My parents didn't drink. They weren't rabid about it, and in fact I remember that when I signed the pledge in grade seven, with the rest of that superbly if impermanently indoctrinated class, my mother said, "It's just nonsense and fanaticism, children of that age." My father would drink a beer on a hot day, but my mother did not join him, and — whether accidentally or symbolically — this drink was consumed *outside* the house. Most of the people we knew were the same way, in the small town where we lived. I ought not to say that it was this which got me into difficulties, because the difficulties I got into were a faithful expression of my own incommodious nature — the same nature that caused my mother to look at me, on any occasion which traditionally calls for feelings of pride and maternal accomplishment (my departure for my first formal dance, I mean, or my hellbent preparations for a descent on college), with an expression of brooding and fascinated despair, as if she could not possibly expect, did not ask, that it should go with me as it did with other girls; the dreamed-of spoils of daughters — orchids, nice boys, diamond rings — would be borne home in due course by the daughters of her friends, but not by me; all she could do was hope for a lesser rather than a greater disaster — an elopement, say, with a boy who could never earn his living, rather than an abduction into the White Slave trade.

But ignorance, my mother said, ignorance, or innocence if you like, is not always such a fine thing as people think and I am not sure it may not be dangerous for a girl like you; then she emphasized her point, as she had a habit of doing, with some quotation which had an innocent pomposity and odour of mothballs. I didn't even wince at it, knowing full well how it must have worked wonders with Mr. Berryman.

The evening I baby-sat for the Berrymans must have been in April. I had been in love all year, or at least since the first week in September, when a boy named Martin Collingwood had given me a surprised, appreciative, and rather ominously complacent smile in the school assembly. I never knew what surprised him; I was not looking like anybody but me; I had an old blouse on and my home-permanent had turned out badly. A few weeks after that he took me out for the first time, and kissed me on the dark side of the porch — also, I ought to say, on the mouth; I am sure it was the first time anybody had ever kissed me effectively, and I know that I did not wash my face that night or the next morning, in order to keep the imprint of those kisses intact. (I showed the most painful banality in the conduct of this whole affair, as you will see.) Two months, and a few amatory stages later, he dropped me. He had fallen for the girl who played opposite him in the Christmas production of *Pride and Prejudice*.

I said I was not going to have anything to do with that play, and I got another girl to work on Makeup in my place, but of course I went to it after all, and sat down in front with my girl friend Joyce, who pressed my hand when I was overcome with pain and delight at the sight of Mr. Darcy in the white breeches, silk waistcoat, and sideburns. It was surely seeing Martin as Darcy that did for me; every girl is in love with Darcy anyway, and the part gave Martin an arrogance and male splendour in my eyes which made it impossible to remember that he was simply a high-school senior, passably good-looking and of medium intelligence (and with a reputation slightly tainted, at that, by such preferences as the Drama Club and the Cadet Band), who happened to be the first boy, the first really presentable boy, to take an interest in me. In the last act they gave him a chance to embrace Elizabeth (Mary Bishop, with a sallow complexion and no figure, but big vivacious eyes) and during this realistic encounter I dug my nails bitterly into Joyce's sympathetic palm.

That night was the beginning of months of real, if more or less self-inflicted, misery for me. Why is it a temptation to refer to this sort of thing lightly, with irony, with amazement even, at finding oneself involved with such preposterous emotions in the unaccountable past? That is what we are apt to do, speaking of love; with adolescent love, of course, it's practically obligatory; you would think we sat around, dull afternoons, amusing ourselves with these tidbit recollections of pain. But it really doesn't make me feel very gay — worse still, it doesn't really surprise me — to remember all the stupid, sad, half-ashamed things I did, that people in love always do. I hung around the places where he might be seen, and then pretended not to see him; I made absurdly roundabout approaches, in conversation, to the bitter pleasure of casually mentioning his name. I day-dreamed endlessly; in fact if you want to put it mathematically, I spent perhaps ten times as many hours thinking about Martin Collingwood — yes, pining and weeping for him — as I ever spent with him; the idea of him dominated my mind relentlessly and, after a while, against my will. For if at first I had dramatized my feelings, the time came when I would have been glad to escape them; my well-worn daydreams had become depressing and not even temporarily consoling. As I worked my math problems I would torture myself, quite mechanically and helplessly, with an exact recollection of Martin kissing my throat. I had an exact recollection of *everything*. One night I had an impulse to swallow all the aspirins in the bathroom cabinet, but stopped after I had taken six.

My mother noticed that something was wrong and got me some iron pills. She said, "Are you sure everything is going all right at school?" *School!* When I told her that Martin and I had broken up, all she said was, "Well so much the better for that. I never saw a boy so stuck on himself." "Martin has enough conceit to sink a battleship," I said morosely and went upstairs and cried.

The night I went to the Berrymans' was a Saturday night. I baby-sat for them quite often on Saturday nights because they liked to drive over to Baileyville, a much bigger, livelier town about twenty miles away, and perhaps have supper and go to a show. They had been living in our town only two or three years — Mr. Berryman had been brought in as plant manager of the new door-factory — and they remained, I suppose by choice, on the fringes of its society; most of their friends were youngish couples like themselves, born in other places, who lived in new ranch-style houses on a hill outside town where we used to go tobogganing. This Saturday night they had two other couples in for drinks before they all drove over to Baileyville for the opening of a new supper-club; they were all rather festive. I sat in the kitchen and pretended to do Latin. Last night had been the Spring Dance at the High School. I had not gone, since the only boy who had asked me was Millerd Crompton, who asked so many girls that he was suspected of working his way through the whole class alphabetically. But the dance was held in the Armouries, which was only half a block away from our house; I had been able to see the boys in dark suits, the girls in long pale formals under their coats, passing gravely under the street-lights, stepping around the last patches of snow. I could even hear the music and I have not forgotten to this day that they played "Ballerina", and — oh, song of my aching heart — "Slow Boat to China". Joyce had phoned me up this morning and told me in her hushed way (we might have been discussing an incurable disease I had) that yes, M.C. *had* been there with M.B., and she had on a formal that must have been made out of somebody's old lace tablecloth, it just *hung*.

When the Berrymans and their friends had gone I went into the living room and read a magazine. I was mortally depressed. The big softly lit room, with its green and leaf-brown colours, made an uncluttered setting for the development of the emotions, such as you would get on a stage. At home the life of the emotions went on all right, but it always seemed to get buried under the piles of mending to be done, the ironing, the children's jigsaw puzzles, and rock collections. It was the sort of house where people were always colliding with one another on the stairs and listening to hockey games and Superman on the radio.

I got up and found the Berrymans' "Danse Macabre" and put it on the record player and turned out the living-room lights. The curtains were only partly drawn. A street light shone obliquely on the windowpane, making a rectangle of thin dusty gold, in which the shadows of bare branches moved, caught in the huge sweet winds of spring. It was a mild black night when the last snow was melting. A year ago all this — the music, the wind and darkness, the shadows of the branches — would have given me tremendous happiness; when they did not do so now, but only called up tediously familiar, somehow humiliatingly personal thoughts, I gave up my soul for dead and walked into the kitchen and decided to get drunk.

No, it was not like that. I walked into the kitchen to look for a coke or something in the refrigerator, and there on the front of the counter were three tall beautiful bottles, all about half full of gold. But even after I had looked at them and lifted them to feel their weight, I had not decided to get drunk; I had decided to have a drink.

Now here is where my ignorance, my disastrous innocence, comes in. It is true that I had seen the Berrymans and their friends drinking their highballs as casually as I would drink a coke, but I did not apply this attitude to myself. No, I thought of hard liquor as something to be taken in extremities, relied upon for extravagant results, one way or another. My approach could not have been less casual if I had been the Little Mermaid drinking the witch's crystal potion. Gravely, with a glance at my set face in the black window above the sink, I poured a little whisky from each of the bottles (I think now there were two brands of rye and an expensive Scotch) until I had my glass full. For I had never in my life seen anyone pour a drink and I had no idea that people frequently diluted their liquor with water, soda, et cetera, and I had seen that the glasses the Berrymans' guests were holding when I came through the living room were nearly full.

I drank it off as quickly as possible. I set the glass down and stood looking at my face in the window, half expecting to see it altered. My throat was burning, but I felt nothing else. It was very disappointing, when I had worked myself up to it. But I was not going to let it go at that. I poured another full glass, then filled each of the bottles with water to approximately the level I had seen when I came in. I drank the second glass only a little more slowly than the first. I put the empty glass down on the counter with care, perhaps feeling in my head a rustle of things to come, and went and sat down on a chair in the living room. I reached up and turned on a floor lamp beside the chair, and the room jumped on me.

When I say that I was expecting extravagant results I do not mean that I was expecting this. I had thought of some sweeping emotional change, an upsurge of gaiety and irresponsibility, a feeling of lawlessness and escape, accompanied by a little dizziness and perhaps a tendency to giggle out loud. I did not have in mind the ceiling spinning like a great plate somebody had thrown at me, or the pale green blobs of the chairs swelling, converging, disintegrating, playing with me a game full of enormous senseless inanimate malice. My head sank back; I closed my eyes. And at once opened them, opened them wide, threw myself out of the chair and down the hall and reached — thank God, thank God — the Berrymans' bathroom, where I was sick everywhere, everywhere, and dropped like a stone.

From this point on I have not continuous picture of what happened; my memories of the next hour or two are split into vivid and improbable segments, with nothing but murk and uncertainty between. I do remember lying on the bathroom floor looking sideways at the little six-sided white tiles, which lay together in such an admirable and logical pattern, seeing them with the brief broken gratitude and sanity of one who has just been torn to pieces with vomiting. Then I remember sitting on the stool in front of the hall phone, asking weakly for Joyce's number. Joyce was not home. I was told by her mother (a rather rattlebrained woman, who didn't seem to notice a thing the matter — for which I felt weakly, mechanically grateful) that she was at Kay Stringer's house. I didn't know Kay's number so I just asked the operator; I felt I couldn't risk looking down at the telephone book.

Kay Stringer was not a friend of mine but a new friend of Joyce's. She had a vague reputation for wildness and a long switch of hair, very oddly, though naturally, coloured — from soap-yellow to caramel-brown. She knew a lot of boys more exciting than Martin Collingwood, boys who had quit school or been imported into town to play on the hockey team. She and Joyce rode around in these boys' cars, and sometimes went with them — having lied of course to their mothers — to the Gay-la dance hall on the highway north of town.

I got Joyce on the phone. She was very keyed-up, as she always was with boys around, and she hardly seemed to hear what I was saying.

"Oh, I can't tonight," she said. "Some kids are here. We're going to play cards. You know Bill Kline? He's here. Ross Armour —"

"I'm *sick*," I said, trying to speak distinctly, it came out an inhuman croak. "I'm *drunk*, Joyce!" Then I fell off the stool and the receiver dropped out of my hand and banged for a while dismally against the wall.

I had not told Joyce where I was, so after thinking for a moment she phoned my mother, and using the elaborate and unnecessary subterfuge that young girls delight in, she found out. She and Kay and the boys — there were three of them — told some story about where they were going to Kay's mother, and got into the car and drove out. They found me still lying on the broadloom carpet in the hall; I had been sick again, and this time I had not made it to the bathroom.

It turned out that Kay Stringer, who arrived on this scene only by accident, was exactly the person I needed. She loved the crisis, particularly one like this, which had a shady and scandalous aspect and which must be kept secret from the adult world. She became excited, aggressive, efficient; that energy which was termed wildness was simply the overflow of a great female instinct to manage, comfort, and control. I could hear her voice coming at me from all directions, telling me not to worry, telling Joyce to find the biggest coffepot they had and make it full of coffee (*strong* coffee, she said), telling the boys to pick me up and carry me to the sofa. Later, in the fog beyond my reach, she was calling for a scrub-brush.

Then I was lying on the sofa, covered with some kind of crocheted throw they had found in the bedroom. I didn't want to lift my head. The house was full of the smell of coffee. Joyce came in, looking very pale; she said that the Berryman kids had wakened up but she had given them a cookie and told them to go back to bed, it was all right; she hadn't let them out of their room and she didn't believe they'd remember. She said that she and Kay had cleaned up the bathroom and the hall though she was afraid there was still a spot on the rug. The coffee was ready. I didn't understand anything very well. The boys had turned on the radio and were going through the Berrymans' record collection; they had it out on the floor. I felt there was something odd about this but I could not think what it was.

Kay brought me a huge breakfast mug full of coffee.

"I don't know if I can," I said, "Thanks."

"Sit up," she said briskly, as if dealing with drunks was an everyday business for her so I had no need to feel myself important. (I met, and recognized, that tone of voice years later, in the maternity ward.) "Now drink." she said. I drank, and at the same time realized that I was wearing only my slip. Joyce and Kay had taken off my blouse and skirt. They had brushed off the skirt and washed out the blouse, since it was nylon; it was hanging in the bathroom. I pulled the throw up under my arms and Kay laughed. She got everybody coffee. Joyce brought in the coffeepot and on Kay's instructions she kept filling my cup whenever I drank from it. Somebody said to me with interest. "You must have really wanted to tie one on."

"No," I said rather sulkily, obediently drinking my coffee. "I only had two drinks."

Kay laughed, "Well it certainly gets to you, I'll say that. What time do you expect *they'll* be back?" she said.

"Late, after one I think."

"You should be all right by that time. Have some more coffee."

Kay and one of the boys began dancing to the radio. Kay danced very sexily, but her face had the gently superior and indulgent, rather cold look it had when she was lifting me up to drink the coffee. The boy was whispering to her and she was smiling, shaking her head. Joyce said she was hungry, and she went to the kitchen to see what there was — potato chips or crackers, or something like that, that you could eat without making too noticeable a dint. Bill Kline came over and sat on the sofa beside me and patted my legs through the crocheted throw. He didn't say anything to me, just patted my legs and looked at me with what seemed to me a very stupid, half-sick, absurd, and alarming expression. I felt very uncomfortable; I wondered how it had ever got around that Bill Kline was so good looking, with an expression like that. I moved my legs nervously and he gave me a look of contempt, not ceasing to pat me. Then I scrambled off the sofa, pulling the throw around me, with the idea of going to the bathroom to see if my blouse was dry. I lurched a little when I started to walk, and for some reason — probably to show Bill Kline that he had not panicked me — I immediately exaggerated this, and calling out, "Watch me walk a straight line!" I lurched and stumbled, to the accompaniment of everyone's laughter, towards the hall. I was standing in the archway between the hall and the living room when the knob of the front door turned with a small matter-of-fact click and everything became silent behind me except the radio of course; and the crocheted throw inspired by some delicate malice of its own slithered down around my feet, and there — oh, delicious moment in a well-organized farce — there stood the Berrymans, Mr. and Mrs., with expressions on their faces as appropriate to the occasion as any old-fashioned director of farces could wish. They must have been preparing those expressions, of course; they could not have produced them in the first moment of shock; with the noise we were making, they had no doubt heard us as soon as they got out of the car; for the same reason, we had not heard them. I don't think I ever knew what brought them home so early — a headache, an argument — and I was not really in a position to ask.

Mr. Berryman drove me home. I don't remember how I got into that car, or how I found my clothes and put them on, or what kind of a good night, if any, I said to Mrs. Berryman. I don't remember what happened to my friends, though I imagine they gathered up their coats and fled, covering up the ignominy of their departure with a mechanical roar of defiance. I remember Joyce with a box of crackers in her hand, saying that I had become terribly sick from eating — I think she said *sauerkraut* — for supper, and that I had called them for help. (When I asked her later what they made of this she said, "It wasn't any use. You *reeked*.") I remember also her saying, "Oh, no, Mr. Berryman I beg of you, my mother is a terribly nervous person, I don't know what the shock might do to her. I will go down on my knees to you if you like but *you must not phone my mother*." I have no picture of her down on her knees — and she would have done it in a minute — so it seems this threat was not carried out.

Mr. Berryman said to me, "Well I guess you know your behaviour tonight is a pretty serious thing." He made it sound as if I might be charged with criminal negligence or something worse. "It would be very wrong of me to overlook it," he said. I suppose that besides being angry and disgusted with *me*, he was worried about taking me home in this condition to my strait-laced parents, who could always say I got the liquor in his house. Plenty of Temperance people would think that enough to hold him responsible, and the town was full of Temperance people. Good relations with the town were very important to him from a business point of view.

"I have an idea it wasn't the first time," he said. "If it was the first time, would a girl be smart enough to fill three bottles up with water? No. Well, in this case, she *was* smart enough, but not smart enough to know I could spot it. What do you say to that?" I opened my mouth to answer, and although I was feeling quite sober the only sound that came out was a loud, desolate-sounding giggle. He stopped in front of our house. "Light's on," he said. "Now go in and tell your parents the straight truth. And if you don't, remember I will." He did not mention paying me for my baby-sitting services of the evening and the subject did not occur to me either.

I went into the house and tried to go straight upstairs but my mother called to me. She came into the front hall, where I had not turned on the light, and she must have smelled me at once for she ran forward with a cry of pure amazement, as if she had seen somebody falling, and caught me by the shoulders as I did indeed fall down against the banister, overwhelmed by my fantastic lucklessness, and I told her everything from the start, not omitting even the name of Martin Collingwood and my flirtation with the aspirin bottle, which was a mistake.

On Monday morning my mother took the bus over to Baileyville and found the liquor store and bought a bottle of Scotch whiskey. Then she had to wait for a bus back, and she met some people she knew and she was not quite able to hide the bottle in her bag; she was furious with herself for not bringing a proper shopping bag. As soon as she got back she walked out to the Berrymans'; she had not even had lunch. Mr. Berryman had not gone to the factory. My mother went in and had a talk with both of them and made an excellent impression and then Mr. Berryman drove her home. She talked to them in the forthright and unemotional way she had, which was always agreeably surprising to people prepared to deal with a mother, and she told them that although I seemed to do well enough at school I was extremely backward — or perhaps eccentric — in my emotional development. I imagine that this analysis of my behaviour was especially effective with Mrs. Berryman, a great reader of Child Guidance books. Relations between them warmed to the point where my mother brought up a specific instance of my difficulties, and disarmingly related the whole story of Martin Collingwood.

Within a few days it was all over town and the school that I had tried to commit suicide over Martin Collingwood. But it was already all over school and the town that the Berrymans had come home on Saturday night to find me drunk, staggering, wearing nothing but my slip, in a room with three boys, one of whom was Bill Kline. My mother had said that I was to pay for the bottle she had taken the Berrymans out of my baby-sitting earnings, but my clients melted away like the last April snow, and it would not be paid for yet if newcomers to town had not moved in across the street in July, and needed a baby-sitter before they talked to any of their neighbours.

My mother also said that it had been a great mistake to let me go out with boys and that I would not be going out again until well after my sixteenth birthday, if then. This did not prove to be a concrete hardship at all, because it was at least that long before anybody asked me. If you think that news of the Berrymans' adventure would put me in demand for whatever gambols and orgies were going on in and around that town, you could not be more mistaken. The extraordinary publicity which attended my first debauch may have made me seem marked for a special kind of ill luck, like the girl whose illegitimate baby turns out to be triplets: nobody wants to have anything to do with her. At any rate I had at the same time one of the most silent telephones and positively the most sinful reputation in the whole High School. I had to put up with this until the next fall, when a fat blonde girl in grade ten ran away with a married man and was picked up two months later, living in sin — though not with the same man — in the city of Sault Ste. Marie. Then everybody forgot about me.

But there was a positive, a splendidly unexpected, result of this affair; I got completely over Martin Collingwood. It was not only that he at once said, publicly, that he had always thought I was a nut; where he was concerned I had no pride, and my tender fancy could have found a way around that, a month, a week, before. What was it that brought me back into the world again? It was the terrible and fascination reality of my disaster; it was *the way things happened*. Not that I enjoyed it; I was a self-conscious girl and I suffered a good deal from all this exposure. But the development of events on the Saturday night — that fascinated me; I felt that I had had a glimpse of the shameless, marvellous, shattering absurdity with which the plots of life, though not of fiction, are improvised. I could not take my eyes off it.

And of course Martin Collingwood wrote his Senior Matric that June and went away to the city to take a course at a school for Morticians, as I think it is called, and when he came back he went into his uncle's undertaking business. We lived in the same town and we would hear most things that happened to each other but I do not think we met face to face or saw one another, except at a distance, for years. I went to a shower for the girl he married, but then everybody went to everybody else's showers. No, I don't think I really saw him again until I came home after I had been married several years, to attend a relative's funeral. Then I saw him; not quite Mr. Darcy but still very nice-looking in those black clothes. And I saw him looking over at me with an expression as close to a reminiscent smile as the occasion would permit, and I knew that he had been surprised by a memory either of my devotion or my little buried catastrophe. I gave him a gentle uncomprehending look in return. I am a grown-up woman now; let him unbury his own catastrophes.

Alice Munro

First Bite at the Apple

I stumbled on Rosie behind a haycock, and she grinned up at me with the sly, glittering eyes of her mother. She wore her tartan frock and cheap brass necklace, and her bare legs were brown with hay-dust.

"Get out a there," I said. "Go on."

Rosie had grown and was hefty now, and I was terrified of her. In her cat-like eyes and curling mouth I saw unnatural wisdoms more threatening than anything I could imagine. The last time we'd met I'd hit her with a cabbage stump. She bore no grudge, just grinned.

"I got summat to show ya."

"You push off," I said.

I felt dry and dripping, icy hot. Her eyes glinted, and I stood rooted. Her face was wrapped in a pulsating haze and her body seemed to flicker with lightning.

"You thirsty?" she said.

"I ain't, so there."

"You be," she said. "C'mon."

So I stuck the fork into the ringing ground and followed her, like doom.

We went a long way, to the bottom of the field, where a wagon stood half-loaded. Festoons of untrimmed grass hung down like curtains all around it. We crawled underneath, between the wheels, into a herb-scented cave of darkness. Rosie scratched about, turned over a sack, and revealed a stone jar of cider.

"It's cider," she said. "You ain't to drink it though. Not much of it, any rate."

Huge and squat, the jar lay on the grass like an unexploded bomb. We lifted it up, unscrewed the stopper and smelt the whiff of fermented apples. I held the jar to my mouth and rolled my eyes sideways, like a beast at a waterhole. "Go on," said Rosie. I took a deep breath ...

Never to be forgotten, that first long secret drink of golden fire, juice of those valleys and of that time, wine of wild orchards, of russet summer, of plump red apples and Rosie's burning cheeks. Never to be forgotten, or ever tasted again ...

I put down the jar with a gulp and a gasp. Then I turned to look at Rosie. She was yellow and dusty with buttercups and seemed to be purring in the gloom; her hair was rich as a wild bee's nest and her eyes were full of stings. I did not know what to do about her, nor did I know what not to do. She looked smooth and precious, a thing of unplumbable mysteries, and perilous as quicksand.

"Rosie ..." I said, on my knees, and shaking.

She crawled with a rustle of grass towards me, quick and superbly assured. Her hand in mine was like a small wet flame which I could neither hold or throw away. Then Rosie, with a remorseless, reedy strength, pulled me down, down into her wide green smile and into the deep subaqueous grass.

Then I remember little, and that little, vaguely. Skin drums beat in my head. Rosie was close-up, salty, an invisible touch, too near to be seen or measured. And it seemed that the wagon under which we lay went floating away like a barge, out over the valley where we rocked unseen, swinging on motionless tides.

Then she took off her boots and stuffed them with flowers. She did the same with mine. Her parched voice crackled like flames in my ears. More fires were started. I drank more cider. Rosie told me outrageous fantasies. She liked me, she said, better than Walt, or Ken, Boney Harris or even the curate. And I admitted to her, in a loud, rough voice, that she was even prettier than Betty Gleed. For a long time we sat with our mouths very close, breathing the same hot air. We kissed, once only, so dry and shy, it was like two leaves colliding in air.

At last the cuckoos stopped singing and slid into the woods. The mowers went home and left us. I heard Jack calling as he went down the lane, calling my name till I heard him no more. And still we lay in our wagon of grass tugging at each other's hands, while her husky, perilous whisper drugged me and the cider beat gongs in my head ...

Excerpt from *Cider With Rosie* **by Laurie Lee**

The Holy Child

The Selfish Giant

The Selfish Giant

Every afternoon, as they were coming from school, the children used to go and play in the Giant's garden.

It was a large lovely garden, with soft green grass. Here and there over the grass stood beautiful flowers like stars, and there were twelve peach-trees that in the spring-time broke out into delicate blossoms of pink and pearl, and in the autumn bore rich fruit. The birds sat on the trees and sang so sweetly that the children used to stop their games in order to listen to them. 'How happy we are here!' they cried to each other.

One day the Giant came back. He has been to visit his friend the Cornish ogre, and had stayed with him for seven years. After the seven years were over he had said all that he had to say, for his conversation was limited, and he determined to return to his own castle. When he arrived he saw the children playing in the garden.

'What are you doing here?' he cried in a very gruff voice, and the children ran away.

'My own garden is my own garden,' said the Giant; 'anyone can understand that, and I will allow nobody to play in it but myself.' So he built a high wall all round it, and put up a notice-board.

TRESPASSERS

WILL BE

PROSECUTED

He was a very selfish Giant.

The poor children had now nowhere to play. They tried to play on the road, but the road was very dusty and full of hard stones, and they did not like it. They used to wander round the high wall, when their lessons were over, and talk about the beautiful garden inside. 'How happy we were there!' they said to each other.

Then the Spring came, and all over the country there were little blossoms and little birds. Only in the garden of the Selfish Giant it was still winter. The birds did not care to sing in it as there were no children, and the trees forgot to blossom. Once a beautiful flower put its head out from the grass, but when it saw the notice-board it was so sorry for the children that it slipped back into the ground again, and went off to sleep. The only people who were pleased were the Snow and the Frost. 'Spring has forgotten this garden,' they cried, 'so we will live here all year round.' The Snow covered up the grass with her great white cloak, and the Frost painted all the trees silver. Then they invited the North Wind to stay with them, and he came. He was wrapped in furs, and he roared all day about the garden, and blew the chimney-pots down. 'This is a delightful spot,' he said, 'we must ask the Hail on a visit.' So the Hail came. Every day for three hours he rattled on the roof of the castle till he broke most of the slates, and then he ran round and round the garden as fast as he could go. He was dressed in grey, and his breath was like ice.

'I cannot understand why the Spring is so late in coming,' said the Selfish Giant, as he sat at the window and looked out at his cold, white garden; 'I hope there will be a change in the weather.'

But the spring never came, nor the Summer. The Autumn gave golden fruit to every garden, but to the Giant's garden she gave none. 'He is too selfish,' she said. So it was always Winter there, and the North Wind and the Hail, and the Frost, and the Snow danced about through the trees.

One morning the Giant was lying awake in bed when he heard some lovely music. It sounded so sweet to his ears that he thought it must be the King's musicians passing by. It was really only a little linnet singing outside his window, but it was so long since he had heard a bird sing in his garden that it seemed to him to be the most beautiful music in the world. Then the Hail stopped dancing over his head, and the North Wind ceased roaring, and a delicious perfume came to him through the open casement. 'I believe the Spring has come at last,' said the Giant; and he jumped out of bed and looked out.

What did he see?

He saw a most wonderful sight. Through a little hole in the wall the children had crept in, and they were sitting in the branches of the trees. In every tree that he could see there was a little child. And the trees were so glad to have the children back again that they had covered themselves with blossoms, and were waving their arms gently above the children's heads. The birds were flying about and twittering with delight, and the flowers were looking up through the green grass and laughing. It was a lovely scene, only in one corner it was still winter. It was the farthest corner of the garden, and in it was standing a little boy. He was so small that he could not reach up to the branches of the tree, and he was wandering all round it, crying bitterly. The poor tree was still covered with frost and snow, and the North Wind was blowing and roaring above it. 'Climb up! little boy,' said the Tree, and it bent its branches down as low as it could; but the boy was too tiny.

And the Giant's heart melted as he looked out. 'How selfish I have been!' he said: 'now I know why the Spring would not come here. I will put that poor little boy on the top of the tree, and then I will knock down the wall, and my garden shall be the children's playground for ever and ever.' He was really very sorry for what he had done.

So he crept downstairs and opened the front door quite softly, and went out into the garden. But when the children saw him they were so frightened that they all ran away, and the garden became winter again. Only the little boy did not run for his eyes were so full of tears that he did not see the Giant coming. And the Giant stole up behind him and took him gently in his hand, and put him up into the tree. And the tree broke at once into blossom, and the birds came and sang on it, and the little boy stretched out his two arms and flung them round the Giant's neck, and kissed him. And the other children when they saw that the Giant was not wicked any longer, came running back, and with them came the Spring. 'It is your garden now, little children,' said the Giant, and he took a great axe and knocked down the wall. And when the people were going to market at twelve o'clock they found the Giant playing with the children in the most beautiful garden they had ever seen.

All day long they played, and in the evening they came to the Giant to bid him good-bye.

'But where is your little companion?' he said: 'the boy I put into the tree.' The Giant loved him the best because he had kissed him.

'We don't know,' answered the children: 'he has gone away.'

'You must tell him to be sure and come tomorrow,' said the Giant. But the children said that they did not know where he lived and had never seen him before; and the Giant felt very sad.

Every afternoon, when school was over, the children came and played with the Giant. But the little boy whom the Giant loved was never seen again. The Giant was very kind to all the children, yet he longed for his first little friend, and often spoke of him. 'How I would like to see him!' he used to say.

Years went over, and the Giant grew very old and feeble. He could not play about any more, so he sat in a huge armchair, and watched the children at their games, and admired his garden. 'I have many beautiful flowers,' he said; 'but the children are the most beautiful flowers of all.'

One winter morning he looked out of his window as he was dressing. He did not hate the Winter now, for he knew that it was merely the Spring asleep, and that the flowers were resting.

Suddenly he rubbed his eyes in wonder and looked and looked. It certainly was a marvellous sight. In the farthest corner of the garden was a tree quite covered with lovely white blossoms. Its branches were golden, and silver fruit hung down from them, and underneath it stood the little boy he had loved.

Downstairs ran the Giant in great joy, and out into the garden. He hastened across the grass, and came near to the child. And when he came quite close his face grew red with anger, and he said, 'Who hath dared to wound thee?' For on the palms of the child's hands were the prints of two nails, and the prints of two nails were on the little feet.

'Who hath dared to wound thee?' cried the Giant, 'tell me, that I may take my big sword and slay him.'

'Nay,' answered the child: 'but these are the wounds of Love.'

'Who are thou?' said the Giant, and a strange awe fell on him, and he knelt before the little child.

And the child smiled on the Giant, and said to him, 'You let me play once in your garden, today you shall come with me to my garden, which is Paradise.'

And when the children ran in that afternoon, they found the Giant lying dead under the tree, all covered with white blossoms.

Oscar Wilde

Authors' Biographies

Anonymous — *About School*

About School was received by David Kemp in 1967. At that time he was told that a fifteen year old Toronto High School student had left the poem on the desk of his English teacher one Friday afternoon. The teacher, finding the poem the following Monday morning, immediately rang the student's home and discovered that the writer had committed suicide over the weekend. The veracity of the story has never been checked. If it is true, the poem is an eloquent epitaph to the young poet, and a tragic reminder of the efforts that must continue to be made to ensure that the school system caters with humanity and compassion to the needs of all the students within it.

Anonymous — *Report*

Report is really a group creation. It was composed by a class of Grade Ten Dramatic Arts students in an English Secondary School. The poem was a part of an anthology presentation on *Authority* prepared by the class. The Drama teacher, Mr. John Bolt, granted permission to include it.

Margaret Atwood *(1938 -   )*

Margaret Atwood, born in Ottawa, is perhaps the most talented poet and novelist to have emerged in Canada in the twentieth century. She creates in her poems a mysterious, threatening dream universe in which she moves as if isolated from all that surrounds her. At times she appears alienated from even herself. Indeed, it is this alienation that enables her to see memories, relationships and the concrete details of everyday life not only as they were, but also as they are changing, taking on disturbing new perspectives. Atwood's world is one of opposites: order and chaos, violence and peace, past and present, life and death, love and indifference. Her clinical, straightforward language seems to serve in revealing the meaning of her poetry both to herself and to her reader. **Death of a Young Son by Drowning** is from *The Journals of Susanna Moodie,* a sequence of poems suggested by the experience of a pioneer in which the themes of alienation and assimilation are memorably portrayed. With many stunning works of fiction to her credit, one of Atwood's greatest contributions has been her analysis of Canadian literary themes in *Survival.*

Jean Beaupré

Canadian Jean Beaupré has worked with English poet Gael Turnbull in translating poems from the French. He has also translated six poems by Paul-Marie Lapointe for publication. For some years, Beaupré worked in the educational system of Ontario.

Hilaire Belloc *(1870 - 1954)*

Hilaire Belloc a citizen of France, was vigorous, lovable and idiosyncratic. A man of enormous physical energy and intellectual vitality, he died at eighty-four, with over 100 books to his credit. His literary output covered a staggering variety of subjects addressed to all sorts of different audiences. In his latter years he often stated that what he wanted to be remembered by was his verse (he would never use the work "poetry" about his own work). He wrote prose, serious verse, sonnets, and epigrams, but perhaps he will be best remembered for his light and comic verse, particularly his verse for children contained in the volumes *The Bad Child's Book of Beasts, A Moral Alphabet* and *Cautionary Tales For Children* from which **Matilda** is selected.

George Bowering *(1935 -   )*

Perhaps more than any other Canadian poet, British Columbia born George Bowering has been influenced by developments in modern American poetry. His style is plain, often mono-syllabic diction with a marked avoidance of abstraction and metaphor. His poetry is characterised by a simplicity of manner which ensures total truthfullness in dealing with the ordinary, the commonplace and the self-evident. Yet, at the same time, there is a wonder at the fullness of the world in which we live. In this volume, the poem **Grandfather** serves as an impressive example of the energy of Bowering's imagination in terms of landscape, men, women and love. In addition to over five volumes of poetry, Bowering's publications include articles, novels and short stories. *Another Mouth* is his most recent book.

Elizabeth Brewster *(1922 -   )*

Elizabeth Brewster, a native of New Brunswick, has published a number of collections of poetry including *East Coast (1951), Lillooet (1954),* and *Roads and Other Poems (1957).* In 1953 she was awarded the E.J. Pratt medal and prize. She has also contributed to various literary magazines in Canada, among them the *Queen's Quarterly, Canadian Forum,* and *Tamarack Review.* **The Night Grandma Died** is her bittersweet reminiscence.

Barry Broadfoot *(1926 -   )*

Barry Broadfoot was born in Winnipeg, a child of the Depression years. During his career as a newspaperman in various parts of Canada he developed a fascination in the Depression and its consequences. In 1971 he left the Vancouver Sun, and with a tape recorder travelled four times across Canada talking to ordinary people about their experiences during the 30's. *Ten Lost Years* is the outcome of these travels. The memories that make up *Ten Lost Years* were collected from more than six hundred men and women. Perhaps the most remarkable aspect of the two excerpts reprinted in this book is their stunning clarity and truthfulness. For those too young to remember the Depression, the experiences recounted are almost unbelievable. Barry Broadfoot has also employed the same technique in dealing with such diverse subjects as the Second World War and the place of the Japanese Canadian in our society.

Charles Causley *(1917 -   )*

English-born Charles Causley's poems are not of the sort that would readily attract the adjective "pioneer." Most of them are, or seem to be, utterly traditional. Yet Causley's handling of ballad and lyrical forms and his jaunty, vivid, humorous way with language seem to lie behind much of the "pop" poetry of the late 1960's, although this is a seldom acknowledged point. His is poetry intended to be spoken aloud, to be grasped immediately and cheerfully by a mass audience. Critic Roy Campbell wrote of Causley several years ago: "His poems have a freshness and spontaneity about them, which, with their fine finish, could never have been attained without the most careful work and subtle refinement." Campbell's insights still hold true. Causley's work has an immediate availability (often to children as well as to adults) which, unlike that of some more recent popular poets, bears re-hearing and re-reading. The rhythms and images work their way into the memory and "earn their keep there." In reflecting on the selection **Timothy Winters,** it is interestng to note that Causley, besides being a poet, is still a practising teacher.

John Robert Colombo *(1936 -   )*

John Robert Colombo is the most active creator of "found" poetry in Canada. In essence, the creator of a "found" poem recasts a piece of prose to reveal something poetic, ironic or otherwise unexpected to the modern reader. Colombo himself has described "found" poetry as a new way of looking at the past, not as it was, but as it is today. In his collection of "found" poetry and literary collages, Colombo displays the happy facility of making unexpected discoveries in the writings of the past and presenting them as arresting entertainments. Although the selection of his poetry in this anthology does not demonstrate what is perhaps his most well known trait, his translation of Jacques Godbout's poem **Enfant** shows him to be a faithful and sensitive translator. Among Colombo's most recent non-poetic works are *Canadian Book of Lists* and *Colombo's Canadian Quotations.*

e.e. cummings *(1894 - 1971)*

Massachusetts-born cumming's work speaks most eloquently to the individual in a stereotyped age. In his introduction to *Collected Poems 1936-1962,* cummings says, "The poems to come are for you and for me and not for most people." His theme is that "Life for most people simply isn't," and he promises 'Never the murdered finalities of wherewhen and yesno, impotent non games of wrongright and rightwrong ..." cummings' poetry itself stands as a statement of his refusal to be stereotyped. In **maggie and milly and molly and may,** we see that not only through the use of unconventional structure and form but even in the technique of typegraphical oddity, cummings expresses his philosophical point of view. His poetry ranges from the intimacy and simplicity of a child's world to acid comments on adult society. One finds savage irony balanced by the most exquisite lyricism. cummings is one of the few successful verse experimenters of our time and one of its truly original voices.

Eloi de Grandmont *(1921 - 1971)*

Born in Baie-du-Fèvre, Quebec, Eloi de Grandmont was one of the founding members of the Théâtre du Nouveau Monde and an actor in the company in its early years. His career in the theatre included work as a director and playwright as well. His play, *Un Fils a tuer (1950)* was written and staged in Paris. Another play, *La Fontaine de Paris (1955),* was the first Canadian play to be produced by the Théâtre du Nouveau Monde in 1955. He wrote many adaptations for the Théâtre du Nouveau Monde, including *Lysistrata, The Fantasticks,* and *Dial M For Murder.* His greatest success was his adaptation of Shaw's *Pygmalion (1968).* As a poet he is less well known. His poems are simple and moving observations on everday subjects: the countryside, the woods, the sunshine, and sleep. His poem **Model Parents** is a striking example of his gift for using plain words to express powerfully his perceptive commentary on universal themes. His collection of poetry *Le Voyage d'Arlequin (1946)* is an elegy for a friend killed in the war. *La jeune fille constellée (1948)* is a mature look that illustrates the poet's delight in simple things. In addition to writing plays and poetry, he also authored *A Guide to Montreal* in 1967, Canada's Centennial.

Paul Dehn *(1912 - 1976)*

Englishman Paul Dehn, a dramatic author, lyricist and critic, is probably least well known for his work as a poet. Between 1951 and 1960 he wrote the lyrics for a number of popular revues, all of which enjoyed considerable success in London's West End. During this time he also wrote the libretti for a number of modern operas which were performed at Sadlers Wells and the Aldeburgh Festival. In addition, Dehn is a noted screen writer. In 1952 he received an Academy Award as co-author of the screenplay *Seven Days to Noon*. He has been the author of such diverse films as *Goldfinger, The Spy Who Came In From The Cold, Murder on the Orient Express* and all four films in the *Planet of the Apes* series. The translation of Jacques Prevert's poem **Exercise Book** shows yet another facet of Paul Dehn.

Charles Dickens *(1812 - 1870)*

When famed British novelist Charles Dickens followed the uproarious fun of *Pickwick Papers (1837)* with the publication of *Oliver Twist* in 1838, many people must have been surprised by his complete change of tone. Yet as G.K. Chesterton said, "The subject of social oppression boiled in the blood of the author." *Oliver Twist,* and indeed Dickens' subsequent works, can be viewed as a campaign not only against social oppression but also against hardness of heart to the existence of human suffering. In *Oliver Twist,* Dickens' crusading spirit is at its highest. His later books, such as *Old Curiosity Shop (1841), Hard Times (1854), Little Dorrit (1857),* and *Great Expectations (1861),* at times stretched pathos to the point of absurdity. G.K. Chesterton says of Dickens, "If he were among us now his revolt would be simply and soley the eternal revolt ... of the weak against the strong."

John Glassco *(1901 —   )*

John Glassco has lived much of his life in the Eastern Townships of Quebec. The rural life of this area is reflected in his poetry which is generally pessimistic and often about nostalgia, loss and the futility of man's struggle against nature. His finest book is perhaps *Memoirs of Montparnasse (1970),* a collection which was hailed as an unusually vivid, highly entertaining, novel-life account of a Paris that was alive with creative people and eccentrics in the 20's. *The Poetry of French Canada in Translation (1970)* was edited by Glassco and was the first anthology of its kind. It contains 194 poems by 47 of the best French Canadian poets, rendered by 22 English Canadian poets. Glassco's translation of Eloi de Grandmont's poem **Model Parents** appears in this volume and is a tribute to the excellence of the anthology as a whole.

Jacques Godbout *(1933 -   )*

Montreal-born Jacques Godbout is a novelist, film producer and poet. He has produced a number of films for the National Film Board, including *Rose de Landry* in 1963 which won the Golden Lion Award at the Venice Film Festival. His films have also won awards in film festivals in Genoa, Rome and Lausanne. He has published a number of collections of poetry and has written one novel, *Salut Galarneau! (1967)* which won the Governor General's Award. He has contributed poetry to several anthologies. In addition, his short stories have appeared in a number of magazines, and his radio and television plays have been presented by the CBC. His sensitively written **Enfant** is included in this anthology.

Moss Hart *(1904 - 1961)*

Moss Hart is one of the best known men in the history of American theatre. He authored the brilliant comedy *The Man Who Came To Dinner* and produced *My Fair Lady.* He wrote some of the most popular comedies to be produced on the American stage and, with scores provided by Irving Berlin, Cole Porter, Kurt Weill and George Gershwin, some if its most memorable musicals. His autobiography *Act One* is a moving life story and at the same time, one of the most authoritative theatre books ever written. In *Act One,* Moss Hart is seen as shy, ambitious, naive, obsessed and hungry, searching for the pot of gold at the foot of the rainbow and miraculously finding it. His description in *Act One* of his childhood struggle against poverty reveals much to us about the quality of the man who was to become the premier playwright of the American stage.

Miroslav Holub *(1923 -   )*

Miroslav Holub is a distinguished research chemist in his native Czechoslovakia as well as a noted poet. Some critics suggest that he is the leading poet of his generation; others feel that this acclaim overstates the quality of his work. Nevertheless, Holub's poetry certainly reflects his scientific training and "often shows us concisely and eloquently the 'uni' in the universe." At times cerebral and glum, Holub supported Dubcek and then "recanted" under obvious pressure. **A Boy's Head** shows him at his most whimsical.

Kate Johnson

Kate Johnson was a pioneer and one of the first prairie settlers in Canada. She wrote of the harshness of the environment in which she lived, as well as the joys and delights of family life. Further examples of her work and indeed, a cavalcade of the reminiscences of prairie settlers can be found in Heather Robertson's book **Salt of the Earth.** Kate Johnson's writing can be found in the Provincial Archives of Manitoba and the extract in this anthology is a typical one.

E. Pauline Johnson *(1862 - 1913)*

E. Pauline Johnson was born on the Six Nations Indian Reserve in Brant County, Ontario, the daughter of an English mother and the hereditary chief of the Mohawks. She was privately educated and attended Brantford Collegiate School. Johnson, whose Indian name was Tekahionwake, wrote extensively about the legends, myths, stories and poetry of the native people of Canada. Her books include *Legends of Vancouver (1911),* and *Flint And Feather (1912)* from which the selection in this anthology was drawn. Two other works were *The Shagganappi* and *The Moccasin-Maker,* both volumes of sentimental tales published in 1913. She contributed poetry and articles to numerous publications in Canada, the United States and England, including *The Week, Saturday Night, Harper's Weekly* and the *Canadian Magazine.*

George Johnston *(1913 -   )*

George Johnston is one of the most readable of Canadian poets. His poems are stylistically light, witty, conversational, and brief, yet they succeed in revealing much about the disturbing qualities of the human condition. Johnston's most well known work, *The Cruising Auk (1959),* is a sequence of poems that explore childhood innocence, domesticity, happiness, adult ineffectualness and doom. His second collection, entitled *Home Free* was published in 1966 and contains two long poems. His translation of Emile Nelligan's **Before Two Portraits of My Mother** is not totally representative of his work; nevertheless, his work shows a sympathy with the melancholy which is so characteristic of Nelligan's poetry. In addition, Johnston's articles and short stories have appeared in many magazines.

George Jonas *(1935 -   )*

Born in Budapest, George Jonas came to Canada in 1956. Since that time, he has worked for the Canadian Broadcasting Corporation in Toronto, first as radio/drama script editor and then as a television producer. In his poetry Jonas pictures modern man as wandering in a vacuum, surrounded by violence and sudden death, lacking permanent values to fortify his existence. *The Absolute Smile (1967)* consists primarily of poems of alienation and loss in which the protagonist leads an unheroic and empty life. *The Happy Hungry Man (1970)* follows for the most part the plain, undecorated style of *The Absolute Smile* but offers some lyric and more positive moments by contrast. Many of Jonas' poems are written in the first person, although his pervasive cynical tone often distances the reader from the characteristi- cally bleak details of his work. His most recent work, written with Barbara Amiel, is *By Persons Unknown* based on the Peter Demeter case.

Ben Jonson *(1571 - 1637)*

Ben Jonson is principally known as an English playwright. His first play, *Every Man In His Humour,* is thought to have had Shakespeare in its cast. It was followed by *Every Man Out Of His Humour* which was performed in the Globe Theatre in 1599. Jonson's finest work was written between 1606 and 1614 and includes *Volpone (1606), Bartholomew Fayre (1614), The Alchemist (1616),* and *The Devil is an Ass (1616).* Although not formally appointed the first poet laureate, the essentials of the position were conferred on him in 1616 when he was granted a pension by James I. Beginning in 1605, he was for many years constantly at work producing "masques", a form of theatrical entertainment which reached its highest elaboration in Jonson's hands, for the English Court. Jonson was buried in Westminster Abbey and the inscription on his tomb "O Rare Ben Jonson" bears testimony to his reputation among his contemporaries, that of an arrogant, quarrelsome, fearless, warm-hearted and intellectually honest man. **My Son And What's a Son,** which appears in this anthology, is taken from *The Spanish Tragedy* by Thomas Kyd and attributed to Ben Jonson.

Irving Layton *(1912 —   )*

Born in Rumania, Irving Layton came to Montreal in 1913 with his family, the Lazarovitches. Critic George Woodcock describes Layton as "an artist in the old romantic sense ... flamboyant, rowdy, angry, tortured, tender, versatile, voluble, ready for the occasion as well as the inspiration, keeping his hand constantly in, mingling personal griefs and joys with the themes and visions of human destiny." Layton's memories of his early life in a slum tenement have been preserved in some of the best poetry, notably in **Keine Lazarovitch 1870-1959** which appears in this anthology. The picture of Layton as a public personality and showman is in many ways belied by the delicate and sensitive quality of some of his work as shown by **Innocence** which is also included in this anthology. A prolific writer, Layton has many volumes of poetry to his credit. His *A Red Carpet for the Sun* won the Governor General's Award in 1959. His most recent book of poetry is *Droppings From Heaven (1979).*

114

Dennis Lee *(1939 -   )*

Canadian Dennis Lee's poetry is in the main reflective. He is one of the founders of Rochdale College in Toronto, and the failure of this free university deeply affected him. In 1972 he published *Civil Elegies And Other Poems!,* a collection characterized by sadness and regret for opportunities lost and moments spoiled. Lee is most widely known, however, for his poems for children. *Waggle to the Laundromat* was published in 1970 and his other books for children *Alligator Pie* and *Garbage Delight* have proved highly popular with both children and adults. **The Bratty Brother (Sister)** is taken from *Garbage Delight.* His most recent book is *The Godo.*

Laurie Lee *(1914 -   )*

Laurie Lee, the youngest of a family of eight, was born in a small Cotswold valley in England. The village in which he grew up was poor, self-sufficient and mainly feudal. *Cider With Rosie,* from which the selections **Village School** and **First Bite at the Apple** in this collection are drawn, recounts his early years. He tells of "thin winters, fat summers, local legends and ghosts, of neighbours and relations, and of growing up against a half-pagan landscape in which violence and madness, country follies and feasts were all part of one pastoral mess-pot." But the time was the 20's and a change was due, although indeed it came late to his valley. Such a world can never be known again; yet Laurie Lee says nothing more than this was how it was.

Gwendolyn MacEwen *(1941 -   )*

To Toronto poet Gwendolyn MacEwen, the big and small events of everyday life have a universal significance that link them to the world of dream, magic and myth. Ordinary experiences take on new meaning as the poet describes relationships between these two worlds by means of metaphor and symbol. Her writing reflects her widespread interests and travel to Middle Eastern countries. She has translated poems from Arabic and has used ancient religions and anthropology as themes in her own poetry. Her works include numerous radio plays, verse-dramas, documentaries for the Canadian Broadcasting Corporation (Radio), and translations of contemporary Greek poetry. She received the 1970 Governor General's Award in poetry for *The Shadow Maker.* Recent works include *Mermaids' Icons: A Greek Summer (1978), Magic Animals (Selected Poems) (1975),* and *The Fire-Eaters (poetry) (1976).* **The Children Are Laughing,** which appears in this anthology, is a senstive yet bitter indictment of an affluent society which has forgotten how to care.

Louis MacNeice *(1907 - 1963)*

The name of Louis MacNeice is invariably linked to those English poets of the 30's, mainly Stephen Spender and W.H. Auden, whose political commitment was stronger that his own. As he said himself, "If the writer is political at all it is his special function to preserve his critical faculty. He must not see things (such as the Spanish Civil War) purely in terms of black and white." He was most at home in his celebration of the ordinary and everyday. Yet he never wrote of these topics with a tongue in cheek attitude. He, better than any other poet of his generation, recognized the imperviousness, except in time of war, of the ordinary man to politics, creeds, and -isms. His sympathy for this attitude is reflected in *Prayer Before Birth.*

Nellie McClung *(1873 - 1951)*

Born in Chatsworth, Ontario, Nellie McClung was a writer, a temperance leader and a champion of women's rights. Her literary career started when she wrote a short story for a *Collier's Magazine* competition in 1902. She expanded the short story into a novel, and it was published under the title *Sowing Seeds in Danny (1908)*. At the time of her death the novel was in its seventeenth edition. *The Second Chance (1910)* and other novels followed, as well as collections of her short stories and sketches. In her sixtieth year, she wrote *Clearing in the West* which is generally regarded as her finest work. **First Day** in this anthology is taken from *Clearing in the West*. A second book of her reminiscences entitled *The Stream Runs Fast* followed in 1945. In Manitoba, where she had moved with her family in 1880, she entered politics as a young woman, compaigning with vigor and mordant wit for social reform and women's rights. She was one of the few women speakers who could fill Massey Hall in Toronto. She sat in the Alberta Legislature as a liberal member for Edmonton from 1921 to 1926. Nellie McClung was the first member of the Canadian Broadcasting Corporation Board of Governors from 1936 to 1942. Her name appears on a plaque at the entrance to the Senate Chamber in Ottawa with those of four other fighters for women's suffrage who succeeded in opening the doors of the Senate to women.

Phyllis McGinley *(1905 - 1978)*

Phyllis McGinley was an American poet, essayist and writer of children's stories. In 1961 she won a Pulitzer Prize for *Times Three Selected Verse From Three Decades*. Proud of her role as a housewife, McGinley often celebrated suburban living with her light verse, but many of her poems bear a serious overtone. She once said, 'My goal is to narrow the gulf between light and serious verse, in the hope that my work will lead my readers into greater poetry.

In addition to the Pultizer Prize, McGinley received honorary degrees from colleges and universities across North America and awards from several literary groups. Her writing career spanned four decades, in which time she wrote eighteen books and contributed to many literary journals, including *The New Yorker* and *Atlantic*. Her poem **First Lesson** reflects her philosphy.

Florence McNeil *(1940 -   )*

Florence McNeil is an accomplished poet and an instructor at the University of British Columbia. In 1965 she was awarded the Macmillan Company of Canada prize for poetry. Her collections of poetry include *A Silent Green Sky (1967)*, *Rim of the Park (1972)*, *Wallachin (1972)*, *Ghost Towns (1975)*, and *Emily (1975)*. Her book *A Balancing Act* is expected in the fall of 1979. *Ghost Towns*, from which **A Grandfather** in this anthology is taken represents an exciting and impressive flowering of her talent. McNeil has her own voice, her own irony and coolness. She writes with an ironic self-mockery that subtlely includes her readers and her follow men and women. By this technique, McNeil establishes herself not only as a poet in her own right, but as a poet in the best tradition of Earl Birney, F.R. Scott and Al Purdy.

Ian Milner *(1911 -   )*

New Zealand born Ian Milner is a poet, translator, critic, and academic now living in England. He has specialised in translations from the Czech and his translation of Miroslav Holub's **A Boy's Head,** which appears in this anthology, is taken from Milner's collection of translations of Holub's poetry.

W.O. Mitchell *(1914 -   )*

Saskatchewan-born W.O. Mitchell is perhaps best known for his novel *Who Has Seen The Wind,* an excerpt of which appears in this anthology. The book was published in 1947 and subsequently was produced as a television film on the Canadian Broadcasting Corporation channel. In 1977, *Who Has Seen The Wind* formed the basis for a very successful feature film. W.O. Mitchell has written extensively for the theatre, the National Film Board of Canada and for provincial repertory companies across Canada. He has contributed a number of radio scripts to the Canadian Broadcasting Corporation, and his works have been translated into many different languages. His short stories have been extensively published both in anthologies and in literary journals. Simon & Pierre Publishing Company Limited published his drama **The Devil's Instrument** in 1973. Mitchell has been awarded the MacLean's Prize for Fiction and the Leacock Award for Humour for his short story **Jake and the Kid** written in 1962.

Alice Munro *(1931 -   )*

Alice Munro's first book, *Dance of the Happy Shades (1968)* from which **An Ounce of Cure** in this anthology was taken, won the Governor General's Award for fiction. Most of her short stories and novels are set in Southern Ontario, in or near a town that approximates the town in which she was born and raised, Wingham, Ontario. The memories of her childhood years have stayed vividly in her mind down to the smallest details, and she uses these with remarkable skill in bringing her characters and background to life. **An Ounce of Cure** is delightful in its utterly truthful re-creation of an incident from the past which is remembered with good-natured amusement as well as notstalgic embarrassment. Her most recent book of short stories, *Who Do You Think You Are?.* won the Governor General's Award in 1979.

Ogden Nash *(1902 - 1971)*

American Ogden Nash was much more than just the good light poet which many re-member. His comments were always in good taste, and they unerringly picked out the foibles, failures and fantasies of man in Western society. His type of satire was as "natural" to twentieth century America as that of Swift was to eighteenth century England. Nash created a world and a language of his own. England's *Observer* newspaper considered his metrical intricacies as "Walt Whitman in delirium". There was within him a philosopher who clothed deep thoughts in frivolous garments. His perceptive, original mind expressed itself with the simplicity of true art, as illustrated in **Song to be Sung by the Father of Infant Female Children** which is included in this anthology.

Emile Nelligan *(1879 - 1941)*

The poetry of Emile Nelligan marks the beginning of modern literature in French Canada. Nelligan's great literary talent is especially remarkable when one considers that all his poems were written between the ages of sixteen and twenty. His poetry often recalled a happy childhood, but his memories, like those of Dylan Thomas in *Fern Hill,* are colored by a strong sense of doom lying in wait for the happy child. Little is known of Nelligan's life or of the source of deep melancholy to be found in his work. We know that he idealized his mother, as is evident in **Before Two Portrait of My Mother** contained in this anthology. Further, he never spoke of his father and suffered unhappiness in his marriage. Some suggest that remarks made by an obscure French critic motivated him to stop writing. In May

1899 he gave what was to be his last reading of his poetry to an appreciative audience at a literary club called Ecole Littéraire de Montréal. Three months later he sank into a depression from which he was never to emerge. He spent the remaining 42 years of his life in asylums and never wrote another line.

Alden Nowlan *(1933 -   )*

Born in Nova Scotia, Alden Nowlan is a regional writer who has his roots deep in the small towns of Nova Scotia and New Brunswick where he has lived all his life. Although his poetry is realistic, he also speaks of the infinite strangeness of our ordinary lives, and he considers the poet to be a kind of magician. Indeed, his poetry has moved increasingly from the realistic into the exploration of the mystery of life. For many years Nowlan worked as a newspaper man, and this no doubt taught him to be direct and concise. He writes in straightforward language which is ideally suited to his clear-eyed, compassioniate view of the world around him. His works include *Smoked Glass* and *Double Exposure Essays*. In addition, he was the co-author with Walter Learning of the very successful play *The Incredible Murder of Cardinal Tosca.* Nowlan's special gift for imbuing the subject of his poetry with warmth, beauty and feeling is well represented in **I, Icarus** and **Roots,** both of which are included in this anthology.

Mary Oliver *(1935 -   )*

Cleveland born poet Mary Oliver lived for some time in England. Her poetry is marked by an emotional maturity and a simplicity of language which auger well for the future. She believes that an affirmation of life is as justifiable as an affirmation of despair. She attempts to marry technique and emotion in order to present simple human truth in such a way that it is conveyed with purpose and clarity to the listener and reader. The themes of her poems are many and include aspects of childhood, the country — both in England and America - and poems of a more personal nature. Her poetry ranges in form from free lyrics to verse which has been likened to the chillingly lovely, formal early poetry of Blake. **The Unicorn** was intended to be spoken at the opening of the Unicorn Theatre for children in London.

P.K. Page *(1916 -   )*

Although born in England, poet, artist and writer P.K. Page came to Canada in 1919 and settled in Red Deer, Alberta. In her early work, Page's poems were mostly on the theme of social protest. However, taken as a whole, her work shows a great variety in subjects. She writes about childhood, dreams, love, innocence and experience, illusion and disillusion-ment, strangeness and terror in technically accomplished poems which are rich with metaphysical imagery. In 1954 she won the Governor General's Award for her book *The Metal And The Flower.* Her many works include novels and collections of poetry, and her poems can be found in numerous anthologies and periodicals. Page has written her feelings concerning the beginning of a poem: "The idea diminishes to a dimensionless point in my absolute centre. If I can hold it steady long enough, the feeling which is associated with that point grows and fills a larger area as perfume permeates a room. It is from here that I write, held within that luminous circle, that locus, which is at the same time a focusing glass the surface of the drum." Her poem **A Backward Journey,** contained in this anthology, is a perfect illustration of this self revelation.

Jacques Prévert *(1900 - 1977)*

Jacques Prévert, a French poet, owes much of his popular appeal to a skilfull blend of satire, humour and sentimentality. His work has been widely translated and can be found in many anthologies and school programs today. During his lifetime, Prévert wrote poems, short stories and collaborated with Marcel Carne in the writing of screenplays. His most well known venture in this field is his screenplay *Les Enfants du Paradis.* His poems were collected in a volume entitled *Parôles (1946).* An instant success, they were soon being sung in Paris music halls and recited in student cafes. The best known translations of his work into English are by Lawrence Ferlinghetti. In this collection, his delightful fantasy about schooltime dreams, **Exercise Book,** is translated by Paul Dehn.

Knud Rasmussen *(1879 - 1933)*

Born in Greenland, the son of a Danish missionary and an Eskimo woman, Knud Rasmussen was perhaps the most eminent ethnologist of his time. He studied the Canadian Eskimos and recorded their songs, poems, legends, myths, and tales. He translated many Canadian Eskimo poems and these appeared in his books, *Beyond the Hills* and *Anerca.* In 1927 he undertook an expedition across Arctic America and his book *A Narrative of the Fifth Thule Expedition* also contains Eskimo poems. Some of these even appear in the official report of the 1927 Thule expedition. The poem **When I Was Young** is reprinted from his book *The Intellectual Culture of the Copper Eskimos.*

James Reaney *(1926 -   )*

Canadian James Reaney is both poet and playwright. He is a Professor of English at the University of Western Ontario, but he has never let his work as a scholar and teacher prevent him from attaining a remarkable degree of productivity as a writer. The experiences of his childhood on a southern Ontario farm, his love of nursery rhymes and fairy tales, his play activities, and the stimulating evangelical religious environment in which he grew up have greatly infuenced his poetry. Reaney's poems, short stories and articles have appeared in numerous periodicals over the years. In 1950 he won the Governor General's Award for non-fiction for his book *The Red Heart.* His play *The Killdeer* won the Dominion Drama Festival Massey medal for playwriting in 1960. *Colours in the Dark,* one of his most satisfying plays, illustrates that in addition to his interest in the world of childhood, Reaney has a larger view in which he sees the world as a metaphor which illuminates powers of symbol and myth. R.B. Parker writes of Reaney, "His sophisticated playfulness depends not only on our recognition of the child, but on our acknowledgment of the adult beneath the child as well. The poet in the mask of childhood. It depends upon an interface between the child beneath the man and the man beneath the child and only when both elements are present do we hear James Reaney's voice in all its complexity." Although **The School Globe,** which is included in this anthology, may be construed as a bitter and angry poem, Reaney's spontaneous playfulness, innovative imagery and dream-like quality are never far away.

Hector de Saint-Denys Garneau *(1912 - 1943)*

Montreal born Saint-Denys Garneau is one of the most highly respected of French Canadian poets. Although at the age of 16 he contracted rheumatic fever which left him with a damaged heart, he was a lively and amusing young man. Nevertheless, his work shows a neurotic capacity for spriritual suffering, and throughout his short life, he became more and more of a recluse. His gift for fantasy is as extraordinary as it is subtle. Garneau had a deep religious faith which coupled with feelings of intense guilt and alienation. His abstract, symbolic poetry grew out of spiritual anguish caused by conflict between a life-loving Christian vocation and an inclination to reject the world. This religious anxiety, and the consequent inner dislocation out of which he wrote, produced poetry, such as **Concerning This Child,** that has been described as "the irreparable loss of inner content." Saint-Denys Garneau is the author of numerous works of poetry and prose, and was a contributor of poems and articles to many anthologies, among them *Oxford Book of Canadian Verse (1960), Saint-Denys Garneau* and *Anne Hebert (1962), Anthologie de la Poesie canadienne-francaise (1963),* and *La Partie, La Presse,* and *La Releve.* His works have been widely translated.

Walter Scott *(1771 - 1832)*

Englishman Walter Scott's initial reputation was made as a narrative poet. Poems such as **The Lay of the Last Ministrel** became immersely popular during the first decade of the nineteenth century. In 1814 he started on a new career as a novelist with the publication of *Waverly.* A succession of novels followed, most of them set in the recent Scottish past. Among the most popular were *Guy Mannering, The Heart of Midlothian,* and *Ivanhoe.* The poem **Cradle Song,** which appears in this anthology, is typical of his romantic and tender style.

Jon Silkin *(1930 -   )*

London born Jon Silkin is an intense poet and the pain of life's experiences is clearly reflected in his work. What he wants to say matters more to him than "niceities" of expression. He struggles to create a sense of "mass" in his poetry and to build his poems up into a coherence so that they will "tell" on the mind. Among his published works are *The Little Time-Keeper* and *The Peaceable Kingdom.* His poem **Death of a Son,** which appears in this anthology, is reprinted from *The Peaceable Kingdom.* It is a personal poem that avoids the traps of sentimentality by its candour and simplicity. Of **Death of a Son,** probably his finest and most direct poem, Silkin writes, "I am attached to the poem; though originally I felt that I should not have written it because it seemed a desecration of the child. It was a poem I could not help writing. The last line went through my mind as my son, Adam, died, and the last line tells you what happened as he died. I felt, or it seemed as though I felt, nothing."

Raymond Souster *(1921 -   )*

Toronto poet Raymond Souster is well known for his witty use of everyday speech. A prolific and accomplished writer, he has many publications and awards to his credit and his poems, short stories and articles are contained in numerous anthologies and periodicals. He is perhaps of all Canadian poets the one whose writing is most closely identified with a single locality, the city of Toronto, where he was born and has spent all his working life. Souster's poetry is unmistakably Canadian. It is about actual experiences and real people, and his poems succeed in arousing true emotions and sharp feelings of recognition. Although his work frequently takes the form of short vignettes or lyrical portraits, his subject matter concerns itself very much with the natural world of love, beauty, jazz, and even poetry itself. He is particularly concerned with the victims of city life, and many of his poems deal with melancholy and nostalgia for times past. He has a reputation for encouraging younger writers and is much admired by his contemporaries. The poems are typical of his work.

Dylan Thomas *(1914 - 1953)*

Writing as long ago as 1936 Edith Sitwell said of Dylan Thomas, "The work of this young man is on a huge scale both in theme and structionally and the form of many of his poems is superb." Dylan Thomas is undoubtedly one of the major literary figures of the twentieth century. Certainly a controversial poet, Phillip Toynbee, writing of Thomas's *Collected Poems* in 1952 said, "Seeing the scope and intensity of the total work it need no longer be eccentric to claim that Dylan Thomas is the greatest living poet in the English Language." But it was not only in his poetry that Thomas revealed his genius. The first twenty years of his life were spent in Wales, and it is of Wales — the people, the legends and the myths — that he writes of with such authority. *A Child's Christmas in Wales* is undoubtedly peopled with aunts, uncles, friends and relatives of Thomas's own childhood. The memories contained in his book *Portrait of the Artist as a Young Dog,* from which the excerpt in this anthology is taken, are memories similarly distilled from his own experience. There has probably never been a poet who is so adept at recalling the magic, mystery, pain and ecstasy of the childhood experience. Dylan Thomas was in every way a unique figure, a giant of a poet. His use of language, his lyricism, and his compassion have yet to be equalled in our time.

Gael Turnbull *(1928 -   )*

Born in Scotland, Gael Turnbull became a physician in general practice and still, in his own words, "doctors to make a living." Although there are undoubtedly American and Canadian influences in his work, for the most part, his life and his poetry are very closely allied with the people and events in Worcestershire, England where he makes his home. He has published a number of poetry collections, including *Poems (1954)* with Eli Mandell and Phyllis Webb, *A Very Particular Hill (1963), Twenty Words, Twenty Days: A Sketchbook (1966)* and *A Trampoline (1968),* from which **And What if,** in this anthology is drawn. His other collections are *I, Maksoud (1969), Finger Cymbols (1972), A Random Sample (1974), Residues (1976)* and *Thronging The Heart (1976).* With Jean Beaupré, he has also translated a number of poems from French Canadian into English, one of which, Saint-Denys Garneau's **Concerning This Child** is included in this anthology.

Miriam Waddington *(1917-   )*

Born in Manitoba, Miriam Waddington's lyrical poems about the Canadian landscape, love and loss, and human relationships are immediately accessible to the average reader. Several collections of her poetry have been published and her poems and short stories have been included in numerous anthologies. She has also contributed several radio scripts for production by the Canadian Broadcasting Corporation. Much of Waddington's poetry shows the influence of the Yiddish language and folklore. Her attraction to tragi-comic experiences and surrealistic images as themes can be attributed to the influence of Hans Christian Anderson's fairy tales on her work. She is fond of the magical in literature and her poetry, while delightfully simple, is endowed with a symbolic and ritualistic element which lies just beneath the surface as can be seen in **Advice to the Young,** which appears in this anthology.

Oscar Wilde *(1856 - 1900)*

The most familiar image of Oscar Wilde does not seem to be that of a man on intimate terms with the sensitivity, beauty and childlike simplicity of his short story **A Selfish Giant,** which is the last selection in this anthology. The mind is much more likely to conjure up a picture of a man who was artist and fop, jester and sage, philosopher and foolhardy adventurer. As an English contemporary remarked, "Oscar is not really well dressed, he always looks dressed up." In a sense the comment is the key to Wilde's personality. He was in disguise. For in truth Oscar Wilde was a magician, a dreamer and a mystic. Above all, he was a born teller of tales. All the magic and mystery of the ancient world lay hidden under that deliberate and ceremonious dandyism. Stories such as **The Young King, The Happy Prince, The Star Child,** and above all, **The Selfish Giant,** are glowing and magical. They evoke the marvels of a world that is all but lost to the mind of modern man, who has placed reason above beauty and material gain above all else, who has banished imagination and replaced it by mere invention. The main question posed by **The Selfish Giant** must be if the story is really intended for children. It is a story that seems to have been written for everyone who is, or who has ever been, a child in the complete sense of the word, for everyone who is fortunate enough or wise enough to have preserved something of what in childhood itself is fortunate, wise and eternal. In that sense it reflects the hope of this book as a whole.

Judith Wright *(1915 -   )*

Born in New South Wales, Australia, Judith Wright spent much of her childhood on her family's sheep station. Her interest in her pioneering ancestry can be seen in her historical memoir *The Generations of Men* published in 1959, as well as in her poetic use of Australia's traditions and landscape. In her first book, *The Moving Image (1946),* Wright begins a persistent poetic search for something steady and reliable in a world which invariably obstructs such discovery. The *Moving Image* is time. In later volumes, especially *Woman to Man (1949),* the search centres on love. Throughout her verse strong intelligence is brought to bear on feminine experience. In 1956 she edited a book of Australian Verse for the Oxford University Press. She is a fine visual imagist and an accomplished myth maker. The deftness with which she draws simple objects or experiences towards symbol by the accumulation of associations raises her to a high level among contemporary lyric poets. **Legend** is perhaps the finest example of this facet of her work.

Dale Zieroth *(1946 -   )*

Critic George Woodcock, in *Canadian Literature,* said of Dale Zieroth, "What Bowering, Mandel and Newlove do occasionally in their poems, remembering prairie childhoods and journeys, Zieroth does in depth with the reconstruction, in images of dark and almost Proustian luminosity, of life in a minority community of a small and remote prairie town." Zieroth writes of the prairie, and it has been said that his evocations of the prairies are some of the best that have ever been written. **Father,** which appears in this anthology, is an excellent example of his gifts.

Acknowledgments

These pages constitute an extension of the copyright page. For permission to reprint copyright material, grateful acknowledgment is made to the following:

PRAYER BEFORE BIRTH from THE COLLECTED POEMS OF LOUIS MACNEICE.
Reprinted by permission of Faber & Faber Ltd.

WHEN I WAS YOUNG translated from the Eskimo by Knud Rasmussen.
Reprinted by permission of Rudolf F. Sand and William Bentzen as counsel for the heirs of Knud Rasmussen.

LULLABYE OF THE IROQUOIS translated by E. Pauline Johnson from FLINT AND FEATHER: THE COMPLETE POEMS OF E. PAULINE JOHNSON.
Reprinted by permission of Hodder and Stoughton Limited.

INNOCENCE and KEINE LAZAROVITCH 1870-1959 from COLLECTED POEMS BY IRVING LAYTON: A GRANDFATHER from GHOST TOWN by Florence McNeil; GRANDFATHER from TOUCH: SELECTED POEMS 1960-1970 by George Bowering.
Reprinted by permission of The Canadian Publishers, McClelland and Stewart Ltd., Toronto.

HIGH HEELS and PARADE OF THE TOYS from DOUBLE HEADER, and BOY PLAYING WITH MUD from TEN ELEPHANTS ON YONGE STREET by Raymond Souster.
Reprinted by permission of Oberon Press.

FATHER from CLEARING: POEMS FROM A JOURNEY by Dale Zieroth; A BACKWARDS JOURNEY from POEMS SELECTED AND NEW by P.K. Page.
Reprinted by permission of House of Anansi.

SONG TO BE SUNG BY THE FATHER OF INFANT FEMALE CHILDREN from VERSES FROM 1929 ON by Ogden Nash, Copyright 1933, copyright renewed 1961 by Ogden Nash. Originally appeared in THE NEW YORKER.
Reprinted by permission of Little, Brown and Company.

DO YOU LAUGH OR CRY and BRIAN ON THE HILLSIDE excerpted from TEN LOST YEARS by Barry Broadfoot. Copyright 1977 by Barry Broadfoot.
Reprinted by permission of Doubleday and Company, Inc.

BEFORE TWO PORTRAITS OF MY MOTHER by Emile Nelligan, translated by George Johnston; CONCERNING THIS CHILD by Saint-Denys Garneau, translated by Jean Beaupre and Gael Turnbull.
Reprinted by permission of Les Editions Fides.

MODEL PARENTS by Eloi de Grandmont, translated by John Glassco.
Reprinted by permission of John Glassco.

ROOTS from BETWEEN TEARS AND LAUGHTER, and I, ICARUS from BREAD, WINE AND SALT by Alden Nowlan.
Reprinted by permission of Clarke, Irwin and Company.

THE NIGHT GRANDMA DIED by Elizabeth Brewster from PASSAGES OF SUMMER.
Reprinted by permission of the author.

MY BRATTY BROTHER from GARBAGE DELIGHT by Dennis Lee; THE CHILDREN ARE LAUGHING from MAGIC ANIMALS by Gwendolyn MacEwen; excerpt from WHO HAS SEEN THE WIND by W.O. Mitchell.
Reprinted by permission of the MacMillan Company of Canada Limited.

ENFANT by Jacques Godbout, translated by John Robert Colombo.
Reprinted by permission of John Robert Columbo.

FIRST LESSON from TIMES THREE by Phyllis McGinley.© 1959 by Phyllis McGinley. Originally appeared in THE NEW YORKER.
Reprinted by permisssion of Viking Penguin, Inc.

MATILDA from CAUTIONARY VERSE by Hilaire Belloc.
Reprinted by permission of Gerald Duckworth & Company Ltd.

ADVICE TO THE YOUNG from DRIVING HOME by Miriam Waddington; DEATH OF A YOUNG SON BY DROWNING from JOURNALS OF SUSANNA MOODIE by Margaret Atwood.
Reprinted by permission of Oxford University Press Canada.

FIRST DAY from CLEARING IN THE WEST by Nellie McClung.
Reprinted by permission of Thomas Allen and Son Ltd. on behalf of the Nellie McClung estate.

Excerpts from the chapters of VILLAGE SCHOOL and A BITE OF THE APPLE from CIDER WITH ROSIE by Laurie Lee.
Reprinted by permission of The Hogarth Press.

TIMOTHY WINTERS by Charles Causley from COLLECTED POEMS published by Macmillan Company.
Reprinted by permission of David Higham Associates Limited.

EXERCISE BOOK by Jacques Prévert translated from the French by Paul Dehn, included in ROMANTIC LANDSCAPE by Paul Dehn.

A BOY'S HEAD from SELECTED POEMS by Miroslav Holub, translated from the Czech by Ian Milner and George Theiner (Penguin Modern Poets, 1967), © Miroslav Holub 1967, translation © Penguin Books 1967.
Reprinted by permission of Penguin Books Ltd.

THE SCHOOL GLOBE by James Reaney.
Reprinted by permission of Press Porcepic Ltd.

LEGEND from COLLECTED POEMS 1942-1970 by Judith Wright.
Reprinted by permission of Angus and Robertson (U.K.) Ltd.

maggie and milly and molly and may, copyright 1956 by E.E. Cummings.
Reprinted from COMPLETE POEMS 1913-1962 by permission of Harcourt Brace Jovanovich, Inc.

Excerpts from PORTRAIT OF THE ARTIST AS A YOUNG DOG and A CHILD'S CHRISTMAS IN WALES by Dylan Thomas.
Reprinted by permission of the publishers J.M. Dent and Sons Ltd., London and the Trustees for the copyright of the late Dylan Thomas.

AND WHAT IF from A TRAMPOLINE by Gael Turnbull.
Reprinted by permission of Cape Goliard Press.

THE UNICORN from NO VOYAGE AND OTHER POEMS by Mary Oliver.
Reprinted by permission of J.M.Dent and Sons Ltd., London.

I WAS AROUND SIX from THE HAPPY, HUNGRY MAN by George Jonas.
Reprinted by permission of the author.

Excerpt from CAMEOS OF PIONEER LIFE IN WESTERN CANADA by Kate Johnson.
Reprinted by permission of The Provincial Archives of Manitoba.

Excerpt from ACT ONE by Moss Hart.© by Catherine Carlisle Hart and Joseph M. Hyman, Trustees.
Reprinted by permission of Random House, Inc.

DEATH OF A SON by Jon Silkin.
Reprinted by permission of the author.

AN OUNCE OF CURE from DANCE OF THE HAPPY SHADES by Alice Munro. Copyright Alice Munro 1968.
Reprinted by permission of the McGraw-Hill Ryerson Limited.